A School Leader's Playbook for Tough Conversations

A School Leader's Playbook for Tough Conversations

Erika Bare

Tiffany Burns

ConnectEDD Publishing

Hanover, Pennsylvania

This publication is available at discount pricing when purchased in quantity for educational purposes, promotions, or fundraisers. For inquiries and details, contact the publisher at: info@connecteddpublishing.com

Published by ConnectEDD Publishing LLC
Hanover, PA
www.connecteddpublishing.com

Cover Design: Kheila Casas

A School Leader's Playbook for Tough Conversations —1st ed.
Paperback
ISBN: 979-8-9933701-2-5

Praise for *A School Leader's Playbook for Tough Conversations*

When I read their first book, *Connecting Through Conversation*, I remember thinking every educator should read it. When I read this one, *A School Leader's Playbook for Tough Conversations*, I thought, *this should be required reading for every education leader.* You did it again! This book is chock-full of both intentional values around conflict resolution as well as practical takeaways. The included sample scripts, guide pages at the end, and helpful summary points at the end of each chapter — all of these together really make this a playbook. Most importantly, these lessons are born from decades of practice, with several vulnerable stories of when Erika and Tiffany get it wrong as well as when they get it right. Thank you for this amazing resource. I can't wait to start recommending it to others!

—William D. Parker | Founder, Principal Matters, LLC

Every school leader knows the tough, stomach-turning conversations that come with the job. This book gives you the playbook to walk in prepared, stay grounded, and come out the other side with the relationship intact.

—Danny Bauer | Host of the *Better Leaders Better Schools* Podcast

A School Leader's Playbook for Tough Conversations serves as a profoundly insightful and vital resource for educational professionals at every stage of their tenure. It masterfully addresses the essential communication competencies that are often omitted from formal training yet remain foundational to the daily demands of leadership. I would have benefited immensely from such a practical framework earlier in my career to navigate the inherent complexities of school administration with greater precision. It is an authoritative masterclass in the nuanced, real-world experience required to lead with clarity, care, and unwavering confidence.

—Steve Mitzel | Executive Director or Operations

This is the book every new school leader needs to have at their fingertips! It's the most realistic, practical guide to communication imaginable for school leaders. With every chapter I found myself thinking, "Yep, I've experienced that *exact* same scenario. If only someone had given me this book, so I didn't have to learn the hard way." Burns and Bare have taken dozens of years of school administrative experience, combined with best practices, and distilled all of that into a fun-to-read, simple guide that will keep any new leader out of hot water, paving their way to becoming the wise, respected leader they are capable of being.

—Dr. Renee Owen | author of *Becoming a Transformative Leader from the Inside Out;* Associate Professor of Education Leadership, Southern Oregon University.

A School Leader's Playbook for Tough Conversations is a must read for new and experienced administrators. The authors combine brain science, real-life stories, and research-based strategies to create a functional resource for educational administrators. Familiar classroom strategies are reframed for use with adults, making them easy to implement and understand. Whether read cover to cover or used as a reference text, administrators will find support for the staff-related challenges they face every day.

—Erikke Nystron-Grothaus | Director of Special Education

A School Leader's Playbook for Tough Conversations is exactly the kind of resource I wish I had years ago as a building principal. Bare and Burns offer a clear, practical roadmap for navigating the conversations we all know we need to have but often don't feel prepared for. While students are always our top priority, this book is a powerful reminder that we cannot truly serve them without having the hard conversations with the adults around them. The real-world examples and ready-to-use strategies make this a book you will come back to again and again. This is a must-read for anyone leading adults in schools.

—Jennifer K. Parks | School Principal

A School Leader's Playbook for Tough Conversations delivers exactly what leaders need: a practical, field-tested approach grounded in real scenarios. Each chapter is organized into clear, actionable segments with strategies leaders can apply immediately—from planning for heated conversations to following through with clarity and purpose. In a profession where the best antidote to anxiety is action, this book provides both the mindset and the moves. Few resources offer this level of clarity and practical impact—this one does.

—Samuel Bogdanove | Superintendent (retired)

A School Leaders Playbook for Tough Conversations is a book I will return to again and again, like a trusted colleague, when navigating challenging moments with other adults in education. As a teacher, I did not anticipate how complex these conversations could be, and this guide offers clear, practical support while keeping the shared goal of better connecting with and supporting students at the center.

—Allison Bingaman | Autism Consultant

Bare and Burns draw from their vast experience as highly successful school administrators to share simple, practical strategies to navigate the countless challenging communications that we face as leaders. This logical guidebook will provide you with pathways to positive outcomes resulting from difficult conversations that you can implement immediately. Within these pages are one "how to" gem after another, including methods of speaking directly and honestly, active listening, controlling emotions, anticipating problems, and solution-based coaching. Throughout, they emphasize that we should ALWAYS stay laser focused on what is best for the kids under our care. The authors exemplify caring, relationship-based leadership in which all parties involved in our students' education are treated with respect, dignity, kindness, and love.

> —Karl Kemper | 35 years as Teacher, Coach & School Administrator

Erika and Tiffany have written another great book that builds so well on their first. They have taken many of the difficult adult conversations school leaders are faced with and applied their insights and compassion to developing practical guidelines readers can use today to improve their communication outcomes. Busy educational professionals will refer back to their useful appendix summarizing communication structures and useful sentence stems. Expect measurable improvements as you practice these principles and communication patterns!

> —Nando Raynolds, M.A. | Licensed Professional Counselor

A School Leader's Playbook for Tough Conversations is a timely and practical guide for anyone navigating the complex human side of education. Grounded in real-world experience, it offers clear, actionable strategies that help leaders approach difficult conversations with confidence, clarity, and care. What sets this book apart is its deep commitment to connection–reminding us that how we communicate with adults directly shapes the environments we create for students. Whether you are a seasoned administrator or an emerging leader, this is a resource you'll find yourself coming back to when it matters most.

—Serena Robinson | Education Leader, Oregon

DEDICATION

This work is dedicated to every school leader currently in the arena. Your courage and commitment are often unseen and, at times, unappreciated. We see you. We appreciate you. We are in awe of you. We wrote this book for you.

Table of Contents

PART II: WHEN THE HEAT IS ON

PART III: COACHING FOR THE BIG MOMENTS

Introduction

No one enjoys a tough conversation. And yet, as school leaders, there's no escaping them. If someone needs to address poor performance or tell a hard truth, that someone is you. School leaders are charged with somehow solving a multitude of unsolvable issues. Most of these require tough conversations, and the unfortunate truth is that these are not conversations we have the luxury of delegating.

We don't know anyone who became a school leader so they could have these conversations. When we met in an administrative program in 2011, neither of us were sure about school leadership. Tiffany wasn't interested in becoming a principal; she wanted to focus on curriculum design. Erika was so happy as a teacher on special assignment that she imagined it would be the role from which she retired. It turns out, fate had other plans for us. Erika is currently a superintendent and has been an administrator since 2012. After serving as a building principal for twelve years, Tiffany now works in higher education and coaches leaders in instructional improvement.

In 2023, we wrote *Connecting Through Conversation: A Playbook for Talking with Students*. Since then, we have been honored to support educators in schools and districts across the country to transform student behavior. We define an educator as *anyone* who has the opportunity to talk with kids at school. We truly believe that at the very heart of education is connection and this drives our mission, which is to ensure that every single student in every single school feels loved, understood, and experiences a deep sense of belonging so they can learn and grow at the highest levels. When we have shared this work with educators across the nation, inevitably, they have turned to us and said, "Yes! This is exactly what I need for the students. But what about the grown-ups? How do I have these conversations with the adults at school?" In answering that question, we became motivated to share what we have learned with all of you.

If you are like us, you made the brave decision to move into leadership for kids, but find yourself spending the most time, energy, and angst on issues with grown-ups. We wrote this book for you. This book is designed to give you a framework, a playbook, a step-by-step guide to having these tough conversations. We are excited to share practical strategies and tools to ensure you communicate with care, clarity, and confidence. We hope this book will not only help you be more effective, but also help you sleep better at night so you can focus on the other ridiculously hard parts of this job.

This playbook is written for busy people, as we've never met an educational leader with time to spare. Our in-depth Table of Contents, clear chapter titles, and headings are meant to help you quickly return to the section you need when you need it. At the end of every chapter, you find a *Connecting It* section that includes a brief summary and a short, bulleted list of *Connected Takeaways*. Throughout the book, we've included helpful strategies, sentence stems, sample scripts, and planning templates. We also included *CTC Tips*–concrete examples pulled directly from our experience. We hope you can learn from our mistakes and successes, so we've shared conversations and scenarios we've had over the years. In all cases, names and specific details have been changed. Combined, these tools are designed to support you during the toughest of conversations.

We know that the excellent communication required for school leadership does not come by accident. It comes from intentional practice, preparation, and time. When we started, there was no playbook for tough conversations at school. No one to tell us to say this, or don't say that. Here's what to say to a toxic teacher, or try this to de-escalate an enraged caregiver, or reason with an irrational community member. We had to figure it out, talk to colleagues, muddle through, and get it wrong–so many times. We had to reflect, rehearse, and review. We can now confidently say while it does not get easy, it does get easier.

Thank you for engaging in these tough conversations. They really do matter. Without them, we are simply unable to build cultures of connection in which students and their grown-ups thrive. Every leader deserves a playbook on how to do this well.

PART I

Strong Communication Starts Here

CHAPTER 1

Say It Because You Care

*"Not everything that is faced can be changed,
but nothing can be changed until it is faced."*

–James Baldwin

Do you enjoy having tough conversations? Is it something you look forward to? We certainly don't. We are guessing that you don't either. We have yet to meet anyone who truly relishes difficult conversations. And yet, as school leaders, we know they are such a critical part of our jobs.

We've all been there. Maybe you need to share some critical feedback with a teacher after an observation, or address some unprofessional behavior from a paraeducator you support. Perhaps there is a colleague or a caregiver who needs to hear a hard truth. None of these conversations sound fun! In fact, they sound pretty hard. So hard, that you might even consider ignoring it and just hope it resolves itself. We wouldn't blame you for being tempted, and yet we know these situations rarely sort themselves out on their own. So, what to do?

Well, start with considering why the conversation actually matters. We know that you are in this work because you care about kids, you care about the adults who serve them, and you care about the school community. When we remind ourselves that we are having the conversation out of care for the educator and the students they serve, it makes diving in and having the conversation a lot easier.

You clearly care about the adults in your organization, so do right by them and share the information that they need to know. When we avoid the conversation, we rob them of an opportunity to improve. And we are robbing our students of the opportunity to have a better experience. Conversely, when we engage, we may even build a stronger connection. We like to remind ourselves to "go to the problem." What we mean by this is, if you have a staff member who needs support, go straight to them instead of avoiding them. In leadership, and life really, the easiest path is rarely the correct one. As leaders, we so frequently find ourselves doing the hard thing because it is the right thing, and these conversations are no exception.

Care Out Loud

If we want people to be open to what we have to say, they must know that we care about them. How do they know we care? We tell them. Out loud. It's always important for us to Care Out Loud, but it's even more important when we need to provide corrective coaching to an educator we support.

Caring Out Loud means that we tell them that we care about and appreciate them. This can be as simple as saying,

"I care about you." The appreciation becomes more meaningful when we share specific reasons *why* we care. As you pass educators in the hall you could say, "I so appreciate the energy you bring to our school" or "We are a better school because of how you help us all build stronger relationships." Develop a variety of ways to authentically articulate how much you care about and appreciate the people with whom you work. Do this early and often, and the impact will be significant.

Caring Out Loud also means that we make the time to get to know the educators with whom we work. When we learn their stories and understand their passions and pain points, we are better equipped to support them. When they feel seen and understood, our coaching is received as a support instead of an attack.

It might feel a bit awkward at first, but the more often you Care Out Loud in genuine ways, the easier it will be over time. What takes very little effort on your part can have a big impact on the person you are talking with. Of course, we can't just say how much we care—actions speak louder than words. We have included a number of strategies to Care Out Loud through actions instead of words in the Appendix. We encourage you to choose one or two to try out. You may want to take it one step further and actually schedule times to Care Out Loud. If you are like us, you'll be more likely to do it if it's on your calendar.

The Message You Send When you Say Nothing

When we say nothing to an educator who is struggling, not only are we impeding their ability to get better, but we are also sending a dangerous message to others in our organization. If you observe a lesson that does not meet expectations, and don't provide that feedback, the teacher has every reason to believe their lesson was solid—no need to do it differently next time. If an educator does something unprofessional, and it goes unaddressed, you are unintentionally setting expectations in the district or school culture that you may not want to live with. In *School Culture Rewired*, Gruenert and Whitaker share, "The culture of any organization is shaped by the worst behavior the leader is willing to tolerate." (2015, p. 36) If you let unprofessional behavior go unchecked, you are letting everyone know that behavior is acceptable in your school or district. If the behavior displayed was problematic and you say nothing, it is not fair to become frustrated when it continues. Speaking of hard truths, that behavior is now on *you*, not them. So, care enough to address the issue directly and with care.

Creating Clarity

When faced with the need for a hard conversation, we often worry about hurting the other person's feelings or damaging the relationship. This makes sense! The feedback may be hard for the other person to hear. However, if we are being honest with ourselves, avoiding this conversation may be more about our comfort than theirs. In *Dare to Lead*, Brené Brown tells us "Clear is Kind. Unclear is Unkind. . . Not getting clear with a colleague about your expectations because it feels too hard, yet holding them accountable or blaming them for not delivering is unkind. Talking about people rather than to them is unkind." (2018, p. 56). If we try to soften the truth too much, we run the risk of the message being lost entirely. If we are not forthcoming with concerns, the hard truth is: we have no one to blame but ourselves when there isn't improvement.

We don't expect students to meet expectations that we did not make clear to them. We share the rules, we provide success criteria, we outline the essential learnings, and we give regular formative feedback. The educators we support deserve the same clarity. If you observe a lesson or unprofessional behavior that does not meet expectations, it is your obligation to provide that feedback clearly and directly. When we don't do that, they don't get better.

> If we try to soften the truth too much, we run the risk of the message being lost entirely.

Don't Wait!

When something is challenging, or decidedly unpleasant, it is human nature to procrastinate. As with most things, the longer you wait, the harder it will be. In the case of sharing critical feedback, the more time that goes by, the less impactful it will be. If there is an area that needs improvement, it should be addressed as closely to when it was observed as possible. This will allow the educator to make a change quickly. Additionally, if someone finds out you have been carrying around difficult feedback without sharing it for an extended period of time, it erodes trust. They are likely to see you as someone who is disingenuous and withholds information. So make a plan, and go have the conversation. We provide a detailed outline of how to build that plan in the chapter, *Planning for a Heated Conversation,* and you can also find our planning guide template in the appendix.

We have all known administrators who don't share critical feedback until a final evaluation conference. This is grossly unfair. Areas for improvement documented in an end-of-year evaluation should never be a surprise to the educator. Formative feedback is as crucial for educators as it is for students. We have even seen times when a probationary teacher was not renewed due to performance without ever being given the information they need to get better. What a disservice to that educator! When questioned, administrators often admit that it felt easier or more comfortable to just not renew than have a direct conversation about what needed to be improved.

> **Formative feedback is as crucial for educators as it is for students.**

Recently, we were speaking with a highly respected veteran principal, who we will call Ms. Bloom. Ms. Bloom shared with us her educational journey, starting with her beginnings as a first-year teacher. Ms. Bloom was hired straight out of her teaching program on a probationary contract as a high school science teacher. As is true for many novice teachers, Ms. Bloom struggled with classroom management. Ms. Bloom was a deeply caring teacher who was passionate about creating dynamic, hands-on learning experiences. Despite her dedication, Ms. Bloom found it difficult to redirect off-task behavior and a few students often created loud disruptions. Ms. Bloom did not yet have the skill and experience to effectively manage the class and, at times, her classroom was chaotic.

After receiving complaints from parents, her principal came into her classroom to observe. The principal noticed many issues and found much to be desired regarding classroom management strategies. Since Ms. Bloom was a probationary teacher, the principal knew she was not required to provide critical feedback nor support in order to non-renew her contract. At the end of the year, Ms. Bloom was stunned and heartbroken to learn that she was not being renewed for the following year. She had lost all confidence that she could do the job she loved and instead returned to her former job as a server at a high-end restaurant.

The following October, Ms. Bloom received a call from Mr. Shepherd, a principal from a nearby district where Ms. Bloom had completed her student teaching. Mr. Shepherd shared that their current science teacher had to take an unexpected leave of absence and would not be able to finish the school year. Ms. Bloom hesitantly agreed to accept the temporary position after talking with Mr. Shepherd about the classroom management struggles she had experienced the year before and asking for support.

With a solid understanding of her challenges, Mr. Shepherd visited Ms. Bloom's classroom several times during the fall. Each time, he shared constructive feedback with Ms. Bloom about what he observed and provided specific ways to improve. He also provided Ms. Bloom with a mentor teacher who helped Ms. Bloom establish routines and strategies to create a more structured environment for her students.

Thanks to the ongoing coaching and support, Ms. Bloom incorporated the feedback and thrived. She went on to become a highly-effective teacher and department head. Eventually, Ms. Bloom was encouraged to pursue administration and spent many successful years as a building principal.

Both principals observed Ms. Bloom's classroom management challenges, and neither principal was bound by the contract to renew her. However, unlike her former principal, Mr. Shepherd actually cared enough to initiate the hard conversations. His feedback was instrumental in helping to cultivate a strong educator. Imagine if Ms. Bloom had never received this critical and constructive feedback–so many would have missed out on learning from such an exceptional educator.

Caregivers

In the same way we cannot avoid sharing hard information with educators we support, if there is something caregivers (our name for parents and primary guardians) should know about their child at school, we need to tell them. In our first book, *Connecting Through Conversation: A Playbook for Talking with Students*, we shared, "Partnering with caregivers is a necessary and important part of our job. This partnership requires that we communicate well, and not hold back information no matter how tempting that may be." (Bare and Burns, 2023, p. 141).

CTC Tip: We encourage educators to connect with caregivers early and often by sharing good news about their child. It strengthens the relationship between home and school when caregivers understand that we know and care about their child. The more positive conversations we have, the easier subsequent tough conversations will go.

It's important that we get in touch with a caregiver when a student displays a behavior that is problematic at school, when they are struggling academically, and when we notice any social issues that may arise. It can be tempting to just try and do what we can at school without involving the caregiver, especially if the caregiver has not reacted positively to communication in the past. We get it. And yet, we cannot let these things slide by without communicating them. Why? Because we care too much about our student's success to withhold information from the most important grown-ups in their life.

When we fail to share information with caregivers, it's bound to come out eventually, and it's never a good idea to surprise caregivers with an issue that we've known about all along. Doing so undermines our ability to build a true partnership, because those actions demonstrate we don't view them as partners. If we want caregivers as partners, we must treat them as such.

When a pattern of behavior is revealed to a caregiver only after the fourth time something happened, it makes sense that they would not believe the school, or they blame the current teacher or administrator. After all, if there was a problem, they should have been made aware right away. Additionally, imagine you are a third-grade teacher and you learn that a student has a pattern of behavior that has gone unreported to the caregivers. You make the phone call, and because it has never been shared, the caregiver blames you. After all, it has

> If we want caregivers as partners, we must treat them as such.

never been a problem before! This isn't fair to the student, their caregivers, or you.

If a student is struggling, we owe it to them and their caregiver to partner with the family early. So, share the data or information without judgement, and provide strategies to support the student both at school and at home. Clear and consistent communication is simply the best way to effectively team with caregivers. We share examples of how to do this in our future chapter on caregiver conversations. We know that our students are far better off when the school and their most important adults are on the same page.

Connecting It

Imagine if there was something you could do to be more effective that was obvious to everyone but you. It is like having spinach in your teeth and going the whole day with no one telling you. The same is true with our performance. We count on others to courageously let us know when there is spinach in our teeth. We must hold ourselves to that same standard.

We know you care about the educators with whom you work. Don't forget to tell them—out loud—so they also know this is true. When you are struggling with stepping into that challenging conversation, remind yourself that you care about them and their students enough to say the hard thing. Choose to be kind by being clear. Take a deep breath and enter into that conversation because you care enough about them to tell them. In the same way, make sure we are sharing all the information with caregivers—the good, the bad, and the ugly.

Connected Takeaways

- Care Out Loud with everyone you support.
- Show you care and engage in those hard conversations.
- It is not fair to hold educators accountable to expectations that you fail to share with them.
- Failing to provide feedback when an educator does something that does not meet expectations communicates that behavior is acceptable.
- Deliver feedback, both positive and negative, as close to the time it was observed as possible. Don't procrastinate.
- Share challenging information with caregivers as soon as you are able.

CHAPTER 2

Feedback Makes an Impact

*"I define connection as the energy that exists
between people when they feel seen, heard,
and valued; when they can give and receive without
judgment; and when they derive sustenance
and strength from the relationship."*

—Brené Brown

Feedback is a gift. We promise. As much as it might feel like criticism, it's the only way we can truly get better. Just as we would never give a student a failing grade without giving them intervention and support, we must take this same approach with staff. School leaders are still teachers. Staff need to know about performance problems early on so they have an opportunity to improve and get support where needed. Being specific and frequent with positive feedback will encourage more of the behavior we want to see, and provide clarity to educators on what is expected.

However, in order for this gift to be well received, our feedback needs to be timely, specific, and actionable.

Timely

What might you say to a teacher who waits four weeks to provide feedback on student assignments? We are guessing that you'd tell them that in order for the feedback to be impactful, students need to hear it a lot sooner. Well, we must hold ourselves to the same standard. When we observe something that would benefit from feedback, we need to share it as soon as possible for maximum impact.

If you are in a meeting, and an educator does an exceptional job of demonstrating the school's values, explaining a concept, or building a strong relationship with a caregiver, go ahead and share that feedback as soon as possible—bonus points if you can do it publicly. Along those same lines, if you observe something that could be more effective with a small tweak, share that right away as well—although, in this case, we don't recommend doing it publicly.

If the feedback is nuanced or requires more significant action on the part of the educator, then it may take some additional preparation on your part. Be sure to take the time to make a plan, but don't wait too long. Ideally, the conversation will occur within twenty-four hours.

If you have been supporting a staff member with something that needs to shift, and you see an example of them either making that shift, or repeating the undesirable behavior, don't wait. Remind them of the conversation you've already had and share the feedback right away.

The sooner we share the feedback, the more helpful it is. When staff know we share feedback instead of holding onto it, it cultivates trust. Conversely, when we withhold feedback and share it later, it feels less like support and more like a "gotcha."

Specific

If we want our feedback to be effective, it must be specific and include examples of observable behavior. Strive to only share objective information–just the facts, please. Subjective information leaves an opening for confusion or disagreement. Provide concrete examples to illustrate what needs improving.

For example, if we told someone they are "negative," this descriptor is vague and has multiple interpretations. If, instead, we provide specific details, it becomes much more clear. Let's say we are supporting a teacher, who we'll call Mr. Bleak. We might say to him,

"Recently, I have noticed a pattern of negativity. For instance, in last week's staff meeting you said that our families would never engage in a family night, so why should we bother. When I sent an email celebrating our dramatic increase in school-wide reading scores, you sent a "reply all" message stating that it was a shame that we were not seeing the same level of growth in our math scores. Finally, I overheard a conversation in which you were discussing the change of policy regarding visitors in the office. You called our district office colleagues 'heartless trolls'."

When being specific, we also want to avoid words like "always" or "never." If we were to say to someone that they are *always* late, they could argue that they weren't late last Tuesday. However, if we share that they were late to work four days last week, it becomes really hard for them to argue with that data.

Additionally, avoid using descriptive words or adjectives. With Mr. Bleak, we may be tempted to say that he was speaking angrily to students. Instead, we might say that we observed him pointing at students and speaking in a loud voice. Sharing observable actions rather than an attitude we perceive, leaves much less room for debate.

Actionable

We also want to ensure folks know what to do with the feedback. Instead of just telling them to "get better," we need to clearly articulate what "better" looks like. Discuss specific actions to take, behaviors to avoid, or strategies to try. Most often, this can be a collaborative conversation in which we brainstorm with the educator different ways to meet the expectation. Of course, there are times when we must be more direct. In our example above, we would direct Mr. Bleak to avoid making negative comments to staff members, and to adjust his tone, volume, and body language when speaking to students and colleagues.

Providing high quality feedback shifts not only the performance of an educator, but also the entire culture of the school. During a particularly challenging time for a school that Tiffany was leading, one senior staff member, who we'll call Mr. King, became rather uncooperative and cynical–focusing mainly on the negative and doing so rather vocally at meetings and in the staff room. The school was faced with some significant budget shortfalls, and it was critical that the educators worked together towards a solution. Mr. King's attitude became contagious, and instead of being solution-focused, discussions shifted to an airing of grievances. Tiffany knew she couldn't just wait and hope that the situation would resolve itself. After carefully considering how to best address Mr. King, Tiffany set aside time to have this tough conversation and followed the steps outlined in our chapter *Planning for a Heated Conversation*.

> Providing high quality feedback shifts not only the performance of an educator, but also the entire culture of the school.

Tiffany began by stating that while he is typically a positive and collaborative leader on staff, lately he had been rather negative and problem-focused. Tiffany gave a few specific examples of times she had observed this occurring. They then discussed the impact his recent attitude was having on school culture.

Mr. King also shared constructive feedback with Tiffany about how she could help make the process of reducing funds easier not only for him, but the entire staff. They brainstormed together how to ensure that future budgetary conversations could be more solution focused. At the next meeting, Mr. King was noticeably more positive and his behavior began to return to a more collaborative style. Afterwards, Tiffany thanked him and shared how much she noticed and appreciated the change. Tiffany also asked for feedback on the changes that she made as a result of their conversation. Sharing this critical feedback was a true turning point in the culture of how the school responded to challenges.

A Balanced Approach

We need to provide a caution here. For critical feedback to be well-received, we must have an established pattern of providing direct and specific praise as well. We are not suggesting the old sandwich technique of starting with praise, saying the hard thing, and then softening it with more praise. This runs the risk of coming off as insincere, or softens the message to such a degree that the meaning is lost, which won't result in the needed change.

Instead, when you see something that is meeting or exceeding expectations, call it out and celebrate it as soon as possible. Be timely and specific. Just as with students, when we praise what we want to see more of, we get more of it. When someone does something that is worth recognizing and celebrating, do it! This should happen far more often than sharing critical feedback.

> **When someone does something that is worth recognizing and celebrating, do it!**

Walk Your Talk

Want to ensure that the staff remains coachable and open to feedback? Walk your talk and regularly solicit feedback on your own performance. Then, model how to use that feedback to improve your own practice, and thank them for it. This creates a culture in which giving and receiving feedback is embedded. Most people are not super excited to share feedback with their boss, so be sure to ask for it directly and let people know how much you appreciate it.

As a building leader, Erika sent a survey each year that asked specific questions related to how she was doing as a leader. Following the survey, she would discuss its results with staff and celebrate things that were going well. Then, she enlisted their help in the areas that needed improvement. She would pose questions like: If my performance were excellent in this category, what would it look like? What are some concrete steps I could take to improve in this area? She would then take that feedback and put it into action.

Another strategy is one we learned from Studer Education: to incorporate rounding into your practice (Pilcher, 2023). Rounding is conducting 10-15 minute conversations with people you supervise and asking the following questions: What is going well? What do you need? Who can I recognize on your behalf?

We recommend adding a fourth question that is specific to something you want feedback on. Rounding has the added benefit of building a culture of celebration and sharing positive feedback. Finally, routinely incorporate the following questions to open the door for someone to share feedback:

- How can I better support you?
- Challenge my thinking on. . .
- I am struggling with x. Do you have any ideas how I could approach it more effectively?
- I would really appreciate your feedback on. . .
- I am feeling like I missed the mark in [that meeting, the presentation, a previous interaction]. Do you have feedback that could help me do better next time?

These questions only work if you truly are open to the response—no matter how difficult it may be to hear.

Remember, this feedback will help you get better, and it is extremely important to model what it looks like to take the feedback and incorporate it into practice. So, when someone gives feedback with the intent to help you improve, always thank them for offering it. Regardless of whether you think it's on point, spend some time reflecting on it. Take action on the things that you can use to get better. Share when you are taking actions based on feedback you received. Let's say you received feedback that you were unclear in staff meetings. Start the next meeting by saying, "I really appreciate the feedback that additional clarity was needed in our staff meetings. Today, I am going to incorporate time when I will ask you to summarize next steps, ask questions, and ensure that we all understand what was discussed. On our meeting feedback form today, I have asked a specific question related to clarity. I would very much appreciate you letting me know if this helped move us in the right direction or not."

Connecting It

We should solicit feedback on our leadership and offer feedback with this mindset as well. For feedback to be effective, it needs to be timely, specific, and actionable. Provide feedback on both what is going well and areas to improve. Leaders set the tone by soliciting feedback on their own performance, and then modeling what it looks like to use that feedback to improve.

Connected Takeaways

- Feedback is a gift. We must share both positive and critical feedback with those we serve.

- Feedback should be timely. Provide it as close to the time it was observed as possible.
- Feedback should be specific. Give concrete examples of observable behavior. Avoid subjective statements and words like "always" and "never."
- Feedback should be actionable. Let them know what action needs to be taken.
- Model how to solicit, receive, and incorporate feedback.

CHAPTER 3

Trust Matters (A Lot)

*"Trust takes years to build, seconds to
break, and forever to repair."*

–Unknown

If you've been in education for five minutes, you know how important trust is. It's necessary for students to learn and it's necessary for staff to thrive. There is simply no possibility of being a successful leader without establishing trust. In *Trust in Schools: A Core Resource for Improvement*, the authors share that when there is trust between educators and their principal, they are more likely to engage in change efforts, participate in problem solving, and trust even, "sustains an ethical imperative . . . to advance the best interests of children." (2002, p. 34) Trust matters.

There are a multitude of excellent books on the importance of trust, how to establish trust, and how trust impacts both culture and results. Although this is not that book, we would be remiss if we didn't share some of the key components of how trust impacts our ability to have tough conversations. The most critical of these elements are dignity, integrity, consistency, and being transparent with our intent.

Dignity

Are we treating everyone with dignity at all times? Do we get to know everyone we serve so they know that we care about them personally? Do we address people by their name, ask about their family, make an effort to get to know them on a personal level? If we can say yes to all of those things, then we are acknowledging their identity, which affirms their dignity. When people know that you will treat them with dignity and respect–no matter the situation–they tend to feel safer around us. This means that we need to be mindful of our daily interactions.

In school leadership, we know that when we speak to an individual staff member, there is a good chance they will share the details of our conversation with others. If you didn't treat them with dignity in that interaction, folks will hear about it, and they'll worry you will treat them similarly. If you engage in gossip, or talk negatively about others, people will assume that you will speak negatively about them as soon as they leave the room. Your interactions in all environments matter. Oprah Winfrey famously said, "Real integrity is doing the right thing, knowing that nobody's going to know whether you did it or not." When we move through the world affirming others' dignity, people will see it, feel it, and be much more likely to trust us.

Consistency

Do you want to know how to tell if someone is consistent? Pay attention to how we feel when we approach them with a request or task. With some folks, as soon as we hit send on the email, we can cross it off our list, knowing they will handle it and follow up when it's done. There are others who we have to make a note to follow-up. Which group do you fall into? Being consistent requires that we do what we say we are going to do, be where we say we will be, follow up, and follow through.

Know when to say no. Being someone others can count on means we can't take on more than we can handle, and we must avoid making commitments unless we are sure we can keep them. This can be especially hard for many of us, as we just want to help. However, saying yes to something we only *hope* we can do sets us up for letting people down. It's hard to trust someone who is inconsistent. Strive to underpromise and overdeliver.

Consistent people show up in predictable ways. We don't want folks to wonder what version of us they are getting today. Folks need to know that we will speak kindly, treat others with dignity, and always lead with our students in mind. We never want someone wondering if they are getting the before-coffee version of us, or the after-coffee version. For Erika and Tiffany, you can rest assured that we never leave home without being properly caffeinated. We know that you are human, and sometimes you may have a bad day or a bad moment. You may respond in a way that is short or snappy. If that happens, you'll need to own up, apologize, and work to make sure that it doesn't become a habit.

Integrity

People with integrity walk their talk. Their actions align to their values. In *Good Leaders Ask Great Questions: Your Foundation for Successful Leadership*, Maxwell (2014) writes about how Gandhi's assistant, Mahadev Desai, described Gandhi. "What Gandhi feels, what he thinks, what he says and what he does are all the same." (p. 131) When all these are in alignment, we know we are acting with integrity.

Showing up with integrity takes courage. It's about doing what is right even when it's really hard. Especially then. If you're wrestling with whether to initiate a difficult conversation, ask yourself what the right thing to do is. If your immediate response is well, it would be so much easier to let it go, consider if this is showing up with integrity.

> Showing up with integrity takes courage. It's about doing what is right even when it's really hard. Especially then.

A surefire way to break trust is by not addressing problem-behaviors in others. When there is a teacher who is incompetent, or is not living the values of the school or organization, other educators know this. Especially our best ones. If we say we must do what's best for kids, and then we fail to hold people to that standard, it's really hard to believe that we mean it. And if we don't mean what we say, how can we be worthy of trust?

Trustworthy people tell the truth. They do not leave out important details or only share part of the story, in any attempt to alter someone's impression of what actually happened. People need to know that they are getting the real story, and not being spun a version of the truth. At the same time, as district and school leaders, we frequently have more information about a situation than we can share, and most often, even if we wanted to share more information, staff and student privacy laws prevent us from doing so. So how do we both tell the truth without leaving out important details and compromising confidentiality? It is tricky, but it typically entails that we clearly state *why* we can't share the information.

Tiffany remembers a time early on as a principal when she was under a lot of pressure from a few caregivers to share the details about a staff member who had recently transferred to another school. As with most of these decisions, the reason for the transfer could not be shared publicly. While the reason was not performance-related, people began to speculate. When responding to the caregivers, Tiffany answered that she believed the staff member would be happy in this new role. Although this was technically true, it left the impression that the staff member had requested the change. The caregivers found out later that the transfer was, in fact, involuntary. The caregivers were furious, and felt lied to—rightfully so. Tiffany felt terrible about the situation, but she did learn quite the valuable lesson. From then forward, when faced with a question that she could not answer completely, she simply responded that due to privacy rules she wasn't permitted to share more information.

These are often such heart-wrenching situations. It is difficult when you have more information than anyone does, and yet, you are judged based on the limited information they have. Do your best to breathe through it and remind yourself that you are doing the right thing. Hopefully, you've built enough trust that folks will also believe you are doing the right thing, even if they don't have enough context to understand. Additionally, we recommend you commit one or more of these sentence stems to memory and use them on repeat when needed:

- I wish I could share more information, but I can't for privacy reasons.
- I know you'd like me to tell you more about what's happening with that situation, but I really can't discuss that further, because it involves confidential staff information.
- I understand your curiosity, but that's not something I can share due to privacy laws and district policy.
- I must protect confidentiality, so I can't go into details about that situation.
- I'm limited in what I can say about that because it concerns personnel matters.
- I can't comment on that specific situation, but I can share what our general process looks like.

Being Transparent with Intent

When we share with someone that they need to make improvements or changes, it must be clear to them that our *intention* is to support their work with students, not to cause them harm. Everyone should know that we are motivated by a desire to do what is best for the students and the community. This means that if our intent is *not* coming from a place of care, then we should pause and rethink.

People are simply not going to trust your intent until they have an opportunity to get to know your character. This can only be demonstrated over time. We encourage you to share your intentions any time an important decision is made, a hard conversation is entered into, or you engage in a new initiative. If we are not transparent about our motivation, others will surely ascribe that motivation to us–true or not. Of course, stating our intentions is not enough. Not only does it have to be true, but it also has to be backed-up by our actions and behavior. Covey says, "While we tend to judge ourselves by our intent, we tend to judge others by their behavior." (2008, p. 79) Strive to consider how the intention of a behavior might be misinterpreted and do your best to clarify. Over time, trust in your positive intentions will come.

> People are simply not going to trust your intent until they have an opportunity to get to know your character.

Erika learned this lesson the hard way when she was preparing for initial goal meetings with teachers in her first year as principal in a new building. Earlier in the year, Erika shared that all teachers were expected to hold high expectations for students and create goals that demonstrated this belief. A teacher who she had worked with previously shared that many believed that because goals were tied to the final evaluation, Erika was trying to get rid of the majority of the staff. Although Erika's intention was for teachers to hold high expectations for students and themselves, she failed to state this clearly. She also failed to recognize that teachers had not worked with her long enough to trust her positive intentions. Erika was able to clarify her intent and set out to demonstrate through her actions that her motives were always grounded in care and what is best for students.

Connecting It

When entering into a difficult conversation, it will go much smoother when we have built trusting relationships. In order to build these strong relationships, we must treat everyone with dignity, be consistent, act with integrity, and be transparent with our intentions.

Connected Takeaways

- School leaders must establish trust in order to be successful in difficult conversations.
- Treating everyone with dignity is foundational to trust.
- Being consistent with our follow through, actions, and in how we show up builds trust.
- Those you serve need to see that you are a person of integrity in order to trust you.
- Being transparent with our intentions builds trust.

CHAPTER 4

Body Position Matters, Too

*"Your body communicates as well as your mouth.
Don't contradict yourself."*

–Allen Ruddock

You are likely familiar with the classic and widely cited study stating that only 7% of what we communicate comes through our words. It goes on to tell us that tone and volume convey 38% of our message, and the final 55% comes through our body language. (Mehrabian, 1971) So, although *what* we say is really important, *how* we say it sends an even stronger message. Let's spend some time examining the ways in which we send 93% of our message so we can ensure that we are communicating what we mean to.

Your Body Is Talking

When we are in conversation with someone, we want to make sure we are at roughly the same physical level. So, if someone is sitting, you should sit as well. If someone is standing, go ahead and stand. In the world of school leadership, everyone already knows you are in charge. You need not flex this power by standing over someone who is sitting, or staying seated while others are forced to stand.

We also want to avoid placing a large object between you and the person you are talking with. When someone has to communicate with you over a big desk, it sends the unnecessary message that you are in charge, and they are not. Instead, we recommend that you sit next to them. Even in the smallest office, you can likely fit two chairs next to each other. If it is really tight, try placing a chair next to your desk instead of on the other side of it.

Much of what we share here we first began exploring under the guidance of Marsha Benjamin-Moyer, long time educator and human resource expert. One of the many things she teaches is to think through where we position ourselves in relation to the person with whom we are speaking. When you can position yourself side-by-side or at a roughly ninety-degree angle to the other person, do it. It's often perceived as threatening or confrontational when we square our shoulders to someone and stand face-to-face. In the animal kingdom this means we are getting ready to brawl. This is one of the many reasons we love a walking meeting. When we can have a difficult conversation on the move, it removes a lot of the pressure simply by moving our bodies together.

If the conversation requires a sit-down meeting, consider a round table if possible. This allows us to sit in community with them without sitting directly across from them. Even if the round table isn't possible, sit next to the person, or at a ninety-degree angle. This also allows you to comfortably share data and look at information together. Similarly, when you are having a meeting with a family, ensure that you do not set up a confrontational situation by having all the school team on one side, and the family on the other. This inadvertently sends the message that it is us against them.

So now that we are in position, what do we do with our hands? We are just a little fascinated by Disney culture. In any Disney park, the employees are not allowed to point. And yet they still have to show people where the bathrooms are and how to get to Space Mountain. Instead of pointing, they gesture with an open hand. This subtle change makes a significant difference. So, when giving folks direction, try an open hand.

We can also send an unintended message with our hands when we cross our arms in front of our body, or place them on our hips. For many of us, this is just a comfortable way to stand. As a tall person with long limbs, Tiffany has to be extra mindful of this. Crossing her arms is just so comfortable and it gives her something to do with her hands. Unfortunately, crossing our arms unintentionally sends the message that we are unapproachable and not wanting to talk. Worse, it can even convey anger or aggression. Try crossing your hands behind your back, letting them hang loose by your side, folding them on the table, or even putting them in your pockets. In Tiffany's case, you'll frequently find her fiddling with a silent fidget (a paperclip, a ring, a squeeze ball). It reminds her to uncross her arms, and it gives her something to do with her hands.

Finally, we have to think about our face. Erika has a notoriously grumpy thinking face. She's been told for years that poker was not the game for her because her face gave her away every time. Over the years, she has learned a few tricks to avoid the resting grumpy face. When she is out and about, she intentionally puts on a neutral or happy expression. When in conversation with someone, she checks in with herself frequently about what her face is saying. By becoming more aware, she is more intentional about what messages her face is sending—and may even be able to win a hand or two of poker. It also ensures that her face isn't giving away her mind's secrets. We are not suggesting people walk around with a big fake smile on their face. Instead, just bring awareness to what you might be communicating, and make sure it matches your intention.

To Look or Not to Look

Erika and Tiffany were raised in a culture where eye contact communicated that we were listening and being respectful. It is not uncommon to hear the phrase, "Look at me when I'm talking to you" from adults at school. We have learned through the years that eye contact is complicated because it's individually, situationally, and culturally specific. An individual's life experiences, neurology, and culture can drastically impact their use of, and comfort with, eye contact.

Eye contact means different things in different cultures. For example, in many cultures, sustained eye contact is considered disrespectful or even rude. Cultural interpretations of eye contact vary widely, so we cannot assume it means the same thing to the person we are talking with that it does to us.

Importantly, individuals who experience some forms of neurodiversity may find eye contact much more challenging than their neurotypical peers. This is powerfully described in *Freaks, Geeks, and Asperger Syndrome: A User Guide to Adolescence*, by Luke Jackson (2002) who identifies as being on the autism spectrum when he says, "When I look at someone straight in the eye, I feel as if their eyes are burning me and I really feel as if I am looking into the face of an alien. I know it sounds rude but I am telling it as it is." (p. 70) If someone is experiencing that level of discomfort with eye contact, it is highly unlikely that they are going to actually hear what we are saying.

Finally, eye contact is situationally specific. When we are under stress, eye contact becomes exceedingly more difficult. When engaging in tough conversations, there is a level of stress involved for both parties. Early in her career, Erika was sitting with her supervisor, who had to share some challenging feedback. Although the information was critical in helping Erika become better, it sure was stressful and diffi-cult in that moment. She remembers how hard it was to look her supervisor in the eye and ended up staring at the desk in between them the whole time. This was awkward for her, and certainly awkward for the person delivering the message. So what do you do instead? We recommend the third point.

The Third Point

Given the complexity of eye contact, having a socially acceptable alternative can be helpful. A third point is an object, most often a piece of paper, positioned between the people communicating. This artifact could be anything–data from an observation, a written complaint, the laptop screen, a printed off record of attendance, an email, or any object that illustrates the purpose of the conversation. As Lipton and Wellman (2002) share in *Learning Focused Supervision*, "physically referencing the third point in a space off to the side between the parties provides a psychologically safe place for the information, concerns, and problems. This careful use of space and gestures depersonalizes ideas." (p. 16)

The third point shifts the energetic weight of the discussion from the people in conversation to the object of focus. So when you are getting ready for a challenging conversation, sit next to the person and place a third point in between you as a safe place for everyone to put their eyes.

> The third point shifts the energetic weight of the discussion from the people in conversation to the object of focus.

Connecting It

Have you ever noticed how easy conversations can be in the car? Children who rarely share more than one-word answers are suddenly opening up. Conversation flows easily between two friends on the ride home in a way that was more challenging sitting across the table at dinner. Being in the car is ideal for conversation because we are sitting side-by-side and there is no pressure for eye contact. Someone has to watch the road! Of course, we can't have our difficult professional conversations in the car, but we can replicate the conditions that make it work. So, when thinking about your next tough conversation, position yourself side-by-side, have a third point in between you, and remember to pay attention to the messages you are sending with your body and your face. All of this will allow the power of your words to come through as you intend.

Connected Takeaways

- The majority of what is communicated to someone comes through our tone and volume and our body language.
- Avoid having power objects between you and the other person, and make sure you are both either standing or sitting.
- Eye contact is culturally, individually, and situationally specific.
- Eye contact is especially challenging when in stressful situations, so incorporate a third point.

CHAPTER 5

Listening for Reflection and Connection

"Dialogue cannot exist without humility."

–Paulo Freire

Have you ever been extremely frustrated, and the person who can solve your problem is clearly not listening well enough to actually understand your issue? We have. Suddenly, we become even more escalated, and our ability to rationally problem-solve goes right out the window. It turns out, before someone can engage in problem solving, they need to know that their point of view is truly understood. As a consequence, when someone is upset, they are likely to continue to demonstrate how upset they are through both words and actions until they can be certain they are understood. This is why listening–and we mean truly listening–is at the heart of communication.

Of course, this happens in schools all the time. If someone comes to us and does not feel we understand their level of upset or their perspective, the way they demonstrate their frustration is often rather unpleasant. In fact, it is typically so challenging, it is hard for us to listen well. Then we get caught in a maddening loop: they do not feel heard, and our efforts to solve the issue are ineffective. The only way out of this upsetting cycle is to ensure that we are listening well *and* communicating clearly that we understand what they are communicating.

> Listening–and we mean truly listening–is at the heart of communication.

Listening well also ensures we are solving the *actual* issue at hand. You know when you talk to someone and they say they are upset about one thing, and it turns out, they are actually upset about something else? As Simon Sinek said in his 2023 YouTube series, *The Art of Listening*, "Listening is not the act of hearing the words spoken. It is the art of understanding the meaning behind those words." This is why we believe so strongly in the old adage: when others get mad, we get curious. When we are listening with true curiosity, we can get to the root of the issue while also demonstrating our desire to understand the other person's perspective. Let's examine what this looks like in practice.

Hear and Be Here Now

It is not possible to listen when our mouth is moving. In order to understand someone else's story, we must give them space to tell it. As Alfred Brendel told us, "The word LISTEN contains the same letters as the word SILENT." So the first step in listening is to be quiet.

We know it's obvious, but couldn't we all use a reminder? When someone is sharing, we need to be sure we are fully present. First, we need to pay attention to the basics. Turning your phone over in conversation often isn't enough. Instead, go ahead and put your phone out of sight and out of mind. This ensures neither you nor the person you are talking to is distracted by the alerts that are sure to come through. We can all be pulled out of the moment when our phone buzzes. It also sends a subtle message that there are other, more important things needing our attention.

Next, pay attention to how present you are mentally. It is hard to keep your thoughts on track, especially when our to-do list is beckoning. We encourage you to practice letting go of thoughts that are unrelated to the present interaction. If in the middle of a conversation, you remember that you still haven't made your dentist appointment, go ahead and jot it down in your notes as a reminder, and then bring your mind back to the present.

This also means we have to listen so we can actually understand what the other person is saying. "To Listen First means not only to really listen (to genuinely seek to understand another person's thoughts, feelings, experiences, and point of view), but to do it first (before you try to diagnose, influence, or prescribe)." (Covey, 2008, p. 214) This is so true—and it is also so difficult. When someone is sharing their version of the story it can be challenging to avoid thinking about how we will respond, or to make judgments about what they are saying. Instead, be very intentional to just listen. Trust that you will know what to say when the time comes. There is no reason to rehearse. When we focus on our response we cannot really listen to what the other person is saying.

Brain science gives us another reason to avoid talking. Did you know that any noise at all activates the amygdala? According to Daniel Gross (2014) in his article, *This is Your Brain on Silence*, published on *nautil.us*, "Noises first activates the amygdala, clusters of neurons located in the temporal lobes of the brain, associated with memory formation and emotions. The activation prompts an immediate release of stress hormones like cortisol." (Gross, para. 11). This is why when we get lost while driving, we need to turn the radio down so we can *see* better! Our voice is simply more noise to someone who is escalated. So, when someone is demonstrating significant emotions, we recommend remaining as quiet as possible.

When considering when to bring your voice into the conversation, we recommend you consider the acronym **WAIT**. This stands for **W**hy **A**m **I T**alking, and **W**hy **A**ren't **I T**alking. It is a helpful reminder to check in with yourself to see if what you are preparing to say will add value or just noise to the conversation. There are times when you absolutely need to contribute; we just want to make sure it is at the right time and for the right reasons.

CTC Tip: The WAIT (Why Am I Talking, Why Aren't I Talking) acronym is a helpful meeting agreement for people to consider when a team is struggling with equity of voice. It reminds people who tend to dominate conversation to give others a chance to speak up, and it reminds those who are quieter to offer more contributions.

Perspective Getting

In *Supercommunicators: How to Unlock the Secret Language of Connection,* Charles Duhigg (2024) introduced us to the idea of perspective getting instead of perspective taking. (p. 110) As leaders, we know the importance of considering multiple perspectives when making a decision. Where we often struggle is in *how* we determine what those perspectives are. We have a tendency to assume we know what the teacher perspective, caregiver perspective, student perspective, and so on, actually are. We may have a good idea, but we can't actually know unless we carefully listen with intention.

As administrators, we were both always careful to consider the teacher perspective. The trick for us was to remember that although we both taught for many years, the second we stopped doing the work day in and day out, we lost that perspective. Similarly, educators sometimes think that because they are also caregivers themselves, they don't need to seek out those perspectives. It's important for us to remember that our perspective is influenced by the fact that we are also educators. So what do we do? Ask questions. The idea is to actually get others' perspectives by asking for them directly. Some great questions you can ask to help with this are:

- I'm curious how you feel about . . .?
- What is running through your mind as I share this idea/issue/etc.?
- What has been your experience with . . .?
- I would love your perspective on this.
- I could use a thought partner, what are you thinking about/feeling as we discuss this?

CTC Tip: A powerful way to learn more about a student's perspective is to actually walk a school day in their shoes. Erika followed the schedule of a ninth-grade student for two full days, and learned so much about the student experience. She then used that information to make powerful improvements throughout the school.

When People Get Mad, Get Curious

When someone shows up extremely angry, a couple of things are likely true. First, they are experiencing the effects of adrenaline, which significantly impacts their ability to think clearly and remain rational. We must remember this in our response, and offer more patience than we otherwise might. Second, it's helpful to remind ourselves that their reaction is about them and, typically, has very little to do with us. Finally, we also need to understand that the issue at hand may be just the tip of the iceberg for them.

Here is a hard truth: anyone has the capability to lose all reason when it comes to their own child. This is why no one should get in between a bear and their cub! Most often when a caregiver is responding with extreme anger, they are wrestling with some extreme fear. Fear that their child is making dangerous choices, fear that they are losing control over their child's life, fear that their child's future is not going to be what they imagine, fear for their safety… you name it.

No one has the capacity to worry like a child's caregiver. So, lean into empathy and remind yourself that this is not about you, and try to get to the real issue. Ask some open-ended questions to try and focus the conversation. A few examples include:

- What would a resolution to this situation look like for you?
- How can I support you?
- What does support look like in this situation?
- What would be most helpful in order to move forward?

When the other person starts to think about what they really want out of the conversation, it can help them focus on the real issue. When the reaction is out of proportion with the situation, you can also gently bring awareness to it. Saying something like, "I can see you are really upset, and I am so sorry about that. I am confident we can work through [name the issue], but I am also wondering if there is more going on here that I can help with?" When a caregiver or staff member is highly elevated about a small issue, that question can help uncover the bigger issue of what is actually going on for them.

Connecting It

The most critical part of any communication exchange is listening well. In order to really hear what someone else has to say, we must be fully present with them and listen first to understand. This often means we need to talk less and listen more, especially if the other person is escalated. When people get mad, get curious. Try and figure out what is at the root of their anger or frustration by asking questions and staying open.

Connected Takeaways

- Be fully present when listening, both physically and mentally.
- Use **WAIT** to determine when to speak, and when to just listen.
- Always stay focused on fully understanding what the underlying issue is. When people get mad, get curious.

CHAPTER 6

Conversation Strategies That Work

"If you just communicate, you can get by. But if you communicate skillfully, you can work miracles."

–Jim Rohn

If you have been hoping for some go-to strategies to approach these tough conversations with confidence, you're in luck. The frameworks we share here are tried and true, and honestly, they just work. As an added bonus, the more we use them, the more natural they become. Once these strategies become automatic, we are freed up to direct our attention to the person in front of us.

Looping for Understanding

Looping for Understanding is a simple technique we learned from Amanda Ripley in her book *High Conflict*. It can be used to both sharpen your listening skills and clearly demonstrate to the other person that you are listening carefully. There are four steps:

1. Ask questions.
2. Summarize what you heard.
3. Ask if you got it right.
4. Repeat until everyone agrees we understand.

The trick to this is to ensure that you are not repeating what the other person has shared word for word, but instead are using your own words and are doing all you can to truly understand their perspective. It might look like this:

Ask Questions	I see that you are frustrated. Can you help me understand more about what is going on for you?
Summarize what you heard	I see. So, the response you received from the teacher was unhelpful and you felt ignored.
Ask if you got it right	Is that right?
Repeat until everyone agrees we understand	OK, so it wasn't unhelpful, but it did feel unkind. Can you tell me more about that?

You can utilize this looping strategy until everyone is on the same page about the problem to be solved. Use it at the start of a conversation. This will surely help minimize conflict when you start to problem solve because it ensures you are both solving the same problem. Additionally, the person you are talking with knows they have been both heard and understood.

The Magic Formula: Acknowledge, Validate, Coach

Think of a time when you felt frustrated or irritated about a situation and you just needed to vent. If you called a friend or loved one and told them about it, how did they respond? Did they listen and allow you space to share your story, or did they jump in with advice and try to solve your problem? If it was the latter, how did it make you feel? We are going to guess that it only increased your frustration. As educators, we do this all the time. We are fixers and we want to help people, so it's understandable for us to want to move right into problem-solving mode. And yet, if we jump to fixing a problem before someone feels heard and validated, it inadvertently invalidates their emotions and their experience. Not to mention that it is rarely effective.

This strategy, coined by licensed psychotherapist and author, Nando Raynolds is called, "Acknowledge, Validate, Coach." (Nando Raynolds, personal communication, December 29, 2022). We find it invaluable in all areas of our lives: at home, with our friends, with our colleagues, and with our students. We find it so helpful that we call it *The Magic Formula*:

Acknowledge: The first step is to acknowledge, or name the feeling that the other person is feeling. Everyone wants to be understood. Letting the other person know that you genuinely see them is powerful. It is important to get this right, so if they are using specific words to describe how they are feeling, use those exact same feeling words as you reflect back what you hear them saying. Of course, they are not always going to use a feeling word, so just take your best guess. If you guess wrong, don't worry; they will tell you. So, if someone demonstrates a lot of frustration, you can simply say, "I can see you are frustrated by this." If they are actually angry, they are likely to say, "I'm not frustrated. I am super angry." Respond with, "Right. You are super angry." There's no need to argue with them about what they were feeling.

Validate: After you have acknowledged the other person's feelings, it's crucial to then validate them. This is the time to assure the other person that their feelings are valid, and you can understand or imagine why they are feeling that way. Even if the feelings seem disproportionate to you, they are their feelings. Just say something like, "It's understandable that you feel that way" or "I see why you feel that way" or "It makes sense to me that someone in your situation might feel that way." The idea is to normalize the feeling and help them feel understood. For many of us, this step is not a natural one. We've even noticed that this is the step folks tend to skip when we practice this strategy during our CTC professional development. Even if you don't agree that someone should be feeling a certain way, we must validate them anyway. After all, a person can't help how they feel. Validating feelings, validates people. We are also ensuring that they feel seen, heard, and valued. It is a

> Validating feelings, validates people.

very useful way to let people know that we take their feelings seriously, and in turn, take them seriously.

Coach: The final step is to coach or teach. This can come only after acknowledging and validating the other person's feelings. We are all educators, so of course we want to move straight into the teaching part. However, if we do this before completely acknowledging and validating the other person's feelings, it will be ineffective and the other person will feel unsupported and unheard.

There will be times when we don't even need to get to the "coach" step. When we give someone space to explain how they are feeling, and we respond by validating that feeling, they are often able to solve their own problem. That is a win. There are other times when coaching is necessary. When possible, ask permission from the other person to move to problem solving. You might say something like:

- This sounds really challenging. Would it be helpful to brainstorm some possible next steps together?
- Are you interested in some feedback about how to address [whatever the issue is]?
- Are you open to some coaching or advice?

Now there are times when we need to offer coaching whether it is welcome or not. In these cases, make sure you have started with acknowledging and validating before you go into that step. Then, you might move into coaching by saying something like, "I get that you are really angry at your fifth period class because of how the students have been behaving. It sounds frustrating. It is totally normal to be angry and frustrated. I am going to share some feedback with you that I am hoping will help get the class on track. My hope is this will help lessen your frustration and help support your students."

When we take time to acknowledge and validate someone's feelings, we are actually acknowledging and validating them as humans. People who feel acknowledged and validated are much more open to coaching, allowing us to work with them productively to a solution.

Compassionate Communication

"When we discuss our feelings, something magical happens: Other people can't help but listen to us. And then they start divulging emotions of their own, which causes us to listen closely in return." (Duhigg, 2024, p. 110) This helps us remember that there are two people with feelings in every communication. When in conflict, sharing our own feelings can be extremely helpful.

Compassionate Communication is a powerful strategy for this. Marshall Rosenberg, PhD developed the principles of Nonviolent Communication, or Compassionate Communication, in his large body of work dating back to the 1960s when he established The Center for Nonviolent Communication. His book, *Nonviolent Communication* provides a thorough explanation of the principles and techniques of this communication approach.

The key to using Compassionate Communication effectively is to focus on your own experience. Speakers put words to their feelings and needs, which leads to a request to the listener. This is in contrast to judging someone else's actions and then making demands on the listener which often leads to more disagreement. For example, if we were to say to someone, "You are always late and it is so disrespectful," they will likely become defensive or argumentative. Notice the difference when we instead say, "I feel frustrated when you are late to our staff meetings." The second example helps get the message across, but we shift the perspective to *how* their actions make us feel. When we focus on our own feelings, the message becomes much more palatable and the person is much more likely to make the needed changes. There are four steps to compassionate communication:

1. Observation
2. Feeling
3. Need
4. Making Requests

Observation: The observation should be a concrete statement of action or fact. It is important we keep the observation free of any judgement or evaluation. We try to avoid adjectives and descriptive words here, which doesn't always come naturally to us, especially in the heat of the moment. For example, instead of telling a child that their bedroom is a disaster, we would say, "I've noticed that there are dirty dishes on the dresser and clothing on the floor." The table below includes examples of observations using Compassionate Communication paired with non-examples that would more likely escalate the situation.

Compassionate Communication Examples	Non-Examples
I noticed you were at your desk during the last four out of five times I have observed you.	You are always at your computer.
I noticed that your gradebook hasn't been updated for the past two weeks.	You are a procrastinator.
I noticed you were not at your assigned duty three times in the past two weeks.	You are never where you are supposed to be.

These examples are all statements of facts, free of judgement, and not something that could be argued with. It is simply a retelling of what you have observed.

Feeling: The feeling statement should be what you are feeling, not what you think about whatever occurred. You can't argue with what someone else says they are feeling. When you do this well, it helps to eliminate the opportunity to argue about the *why* of the request, and reduces the chance of escalating the conflict. The feeling statement also does not indicate what we believe others know, think, or feel. A true feelings statement is not, "I feel like you are not taking this seriously" or "I feel like you know better." These are not feeling statements. These are judgment statements. A true feelings statement following an observation sounds like this:

- "I noticed you were at your desk during the passing period the last four out of five times I have observed you. I feel nervous, because we are counting on you to provide the needed supervision during this time."
- "Your gradebook was last updated two weeks ago. I feel concerned, because we have told families and students that it will be updated weekly."
- "I noticed you were not at your assigned duty three times in the past two weeks. This makes me feel frustrated, because this meant your colleagues had to cover for you."

Need: This is a statement about how your feeling is driven by a need. So, as school leaders, we need to make sure all students are learning, that there is an orderly safe environment, that we are communicating clearly, and so on. When we match our feeling to a need, it helps the other person see that it is not an arbitrary or unreasonable request. So, with the above situations, let's add our need to the feeling statements.

- "I noticed you were at your desk during the passing period the last four out of five times I have observed you. I feel nervous, because we are counting on you to provide the needed supervision during this time. I need to make sure that all our students are safe and well supervised."
- "Your gradebook was last updated two weeks ago. I feel concerned, because we have told families and

students that it will be updated weekly. I need to make sure that we are consistently keeping our students and families up to date on how they are doing."

- "I noticed you were not at your assigned duty three times in the past two weeks. This makes me feel frustrated, because this meant your colleagues had to cover for you. I need to make sure that everyone is able to focus on their own responsibilities."

Request: Finally, we want to partner with the person we are talking with to solve the problem. This is when we share what we would like the other person to do to help meet our needs. These requests need to be both concrete and possible. When adding this final step, we have the following:

- "I noticed you were at your desk during the passing period the last four out of five times I have observed you. I feel nervous, because we are counting on you to provide the needed supervision during this time. I need to make sure that all our students are safe and well supervised. Are you willing to commit to being present during the passing periods?"
- "Your gradebook was last updated two weeks ago. I feel concerned, because we have told families and students that it will be updated weekly. I need to make sure that we are consistently keeping our students and families up to date on how they are doing. Are you open to sitting down with the instructional coach to identify ways to do this more efficiently so you don't get behind?"
- "I noticed you were not at your assigned duty three times in the past two weeks. This makes me feel

frustrated, because this meant your colleagues had to cover for you. I need to make sure that everyone is able to focus on their own responsibilities. You indicated that you are losing track of time. Are you open to discussing strategies for staying on schedule?"

As leaders, we often add a last step here. It can be quite helpful to follow up that request with another question: What support do you need? This simple question helps to ensure that our staff knows they have our support in making the needed changes and shows our willingness to work alongside them.

Connecting It

Incorporate some go-to strategies into your tough conversations—and even those that are not that tough. They provide frameworks that help to ensure our conversations go well. Looping for Understanding helps ensure that the other person feels heard and understood. Acknowledge, Validate, Coach is such a powerful strategy, we call it the Magic Formula! Compassionate Communication is our go-to strategy for problem solving.

Connected Takeaways

- Looping for Understanding helps you listen well, and demonstrates your understanding to the other person. There are four steps: Ask questions, summarize what you heard, ask if you got it right, repeat until everyone agrees we understand.

- When someone is expressing emotion, use Acknowledge, Validate, Coach to empathetically demonstrate listening and understanding.
- Compassionate Communication is a helpful problem-solving strategy that improves listening by sharing feelings through these four steps: observation, feeling, need, request.

When the Heat is On

CHAPTER 7

Keeping Your Cool

*"If you can't get yourself right, you'll have
a hard time getting dialogue right."*

–Kim Scott *Radical Candor* (2017, p. 33)

In both work and life, a frustrating truth is that the only thing we can actually control is ourselves. This is especially true in stressful situations. Some situations feel stressful simply because they are out of our control. When we are in conflict with someone, we may even find ourselves trying to wrestle for control. However, this can be destructive, and certainly does not cultivate connection. When we engage in tough conversations, it's best to focus on the only thing that is truly within our own control: ourselves. If we are able to maintain composure, respond thoughtfully, and keep our emotions in check, then, even if the situation doesn't go the way we wanted, at the very least, we can feel successful knowing that we managed ourselves to the best of our abilities. This is so much easier said than done, but it does get easier with awareness and practice, so let's dive in.

Emotions are Contagious

Imagine your work bestie calls you with really exciting news about a project they got approved. They are over the moon, and full of excitement. Even if you were in a so-so mood before the conversation, you are likely to leave it feeling uplifted and excited as

> When we engage in tough conversations, it's best to focus on the only thing that is truly within our own control: ourselves.

well. Now, think about the last time you were in a conversation with some colleagues who were feeling negative about something happening at the district office. They were frustrated, worried, and all-around upset. Regardless of how you felt about the situation before the conversation, you probably left the interaction feeling negative. In both cases, you caught their emotion.

We have all experienced this contagion of emotions. As it turns out, there is a science behind this. We all have mirror neurons, which is how our body helps us empathize and connect with others. According to an article by Lea Winerman (2005) of American Psychological Association, "Mirror neurons are a type of brain cell that responds equally when we perform an action and when we witness someone else perform the same action." Hammond (2014) applies this information in education in her book *Culturally Responsive Teaching and the Brain*, "To make sure we connect with others, our brains developed mirror neurons to keep in sync with each other. Mirror neurons are special brain cells that prompt us to mimic others." (2014, p. 74) In this sense, humans are hardwired for connection. This often shows up when we subconsciously match the tone and energy of others that is driven by our human instinct to connect.

Knowing this, it's helpful to use the power of this contagion of emotions for the good. When the person we are speaking with is exceptionally angry, it would be easy to match that emotion and respond with anger of our own, escalating the situation further. When we do this, it's important not to blame or shame ourselves. Instead, we can simply bring our awareness to it and intentionally unmatch. We do this by planting our feet firmly on the ground, taking some deep breaths, and recognizing that this is their emotion, not ours. If they go higher and louder, we go lower and slower. We remind ourselves to intentionally unmatch, slow our breathing and our speech, and maintain our calm. After all, the contagion of emotions works both ways. There is a good chance they will catch our calm.

Make Sure You're Ready

When we know we must have a tough conversation about something someone did that was inappropriate or unsafe, you may experience some pretty strong emotions. You may even be frustrated or furious. It is critical in these moments that you check in with yourself and make sure you are in the right head space to engage. Perhaps you need to take a walk. Maybe you need to sleep on it. You might need to reframe and remember that you do not have all the information yet and should suspend judgement. Regardless, if you are still angry, you are not ready. Leaders tend to be task-oriented and driven to cross things off their list. In these situations, waiting until you are truly ready will save you time and heartache. There are so few cases when the conversation must happen immediately. Give yourself permission to wait, and have the conversation at a time when you can engage more productively.

This may also be an important time to get clear on your motivation for having the conversation. Remember, the purpose of every conversation must be rooted in care. Care for the other person, care for students, care for the school or organization. It cannot stem from a desire to put the other person in their place, or show them who is really in charge. When our motivation is off, we tend to say things we regret—and we are not usually proud of how we acted. So, slow down. We are not recommending you skip the conversation—in fact, if you have such a strong emotional response, it's usually a sign that you *must* have it. Just make sure you are emotionally ready before you do.

There was a time that Erika observed a teacher respond to a child with exceptionalities in a way that was unacceptable. She intervened on the student's behalf in the moment and then walked away. Erika was really, really angry. In fact, she was furious. It would not be surprising if there was steam coming off her as she walked away. After class, the teacher came to her office to talk about it. Erika knew she was not ready, and she said so. She acknowledged the teacher and thanked him for seeking her out to talk about it, but Erika shared that she was not ready. In effect she said, "Honestly, I am too angry and upset to talk about it right now. I need a little bit of time before I can engage in a productive conversation. I will arrange a time tomorrow when I am feeling calmer." This did a few things. One, it modeled what to do when your emotions are not where they need to be in order to have a positive conversation, which was something this teacher needed to see. Sharing her emotional response also clearly communicated the seriousness of the situation. Additionally, it gave Erika enough time to get emotionally ready to engage with the teacher and think rationally about next steps. In this case, there needed to be disciplinary action and some significant follow up. Had Erika responded immediately, the focus would have been on Erika's lack of emotional regulation, instead of the inappropriate behavior of the teacher.

Connecting It

Emotions are contagious. Connected Communicators recognize this so that they can avoid catching the negative emotions they don't want, and can focus on helping others catch their calm. Before engaging in a conversation, be clear on your motivation and ensure you are in the right headspace to have a productive conversation. If you are not ready—wait. You don't want to do or say something that you will regret. When we truly consider the power of emotions, we are able to have conversations that build, instead of break, connection.

> When we truly consider the power of emotions, we are able to have conversations that build, instead of break, connection.

Connected Takeaways

- Emotions are contagious—make sure yours are worth catching.

- When you notice that you've caught someone's emotions, intentionally unmatch by planting your feet, taking deep breaths, and bringing your awareness to your response.
- When someone speaks higher and faster, go lower and slower.
- Ensure you are clear on your motivation and in control of your emotions before you engage in a conversation with someone.

CHAPTER 8

Handling the Heat in Unexpected Conversations

"Sometimes you can defuse a difficult situation simply by being willing to understand the other person. Often all that people need is to know that someone else cares about how they feel and is attempting to understand their position."

-Brian Tracy

It has happened to all of us. You are going about your day, focused on the important work that you have scheduled, and suddenly there is an angry caregiver or frustrated educator demanding to talk about their concern—*right now*. This is quite simply not fun, and can understandably cause some anxiety. In these moments, having some go-to strategies can help de-escalate a conflict before it takes on a life of its own.

Focus on You First

As we discussed in the previous chapter, when someone is escalated, it is critical to avoid catching their emotions. Instead, focus on your own calm and remember—emotions are contagious. It is easy to match anger with anger, or frustration with frustration. Instead, take a few deep breaths, get a sip of water, and focus on maintaining (or finding) calm.

This is also a great time to take a moment to remind yourself this is not about you. It is not personal, even though it may feel that way. In your mind, separate yourself from the problem and put it on the table in front of you. If necessary, remind yourself and whomever you are talking with to keep the conversation focused on solutions and not individuals.

> **CTC Tip:** Tiffany never goes anywhere without her water. When things start to heat up, she takes a drink of water and uses that moment to return her attention to her breath—and her feet. She is able to stay regulated as long as she remembers to breathe and keep her feet planted firmly on the ground.

What Is this Really About?

Oftentimes the stated issue is not the real cause of the upset at all. It is part of our job in these situations to identify the angst under the anger. Ask yourself, what is this really about? Then, get curious and listen carefully.

With caregivers, oftentimes the underlying emotion they are experiencing is fear. It is hard to relinquish control of their child's life for the six hours they are away at school. Anger is often an easier emotion to face than fear—especially when it has to do with their own child. When we recognize that anger is often just worry in disguise, it is far easier to problem solve.

> When we recognize that anger is often just worry in disguise, it is far easier to problem solve.

With educators, the stated issue is often a placeholder for a bigger concern. For example, they may indicate they are frustrated by a co-workers engagement in their Professional Learning Community (PLC), but what they are really worried about is that the other educator is getting better results and they don't know what to do. So, as Ted Lasso would say, "Be curious, not judgmental." Ask them, "What is most challenging about this situation for you?" or "I sense there are layers to this issue. Is there anything else I should know about?" Once we fully understand the real issue, we can work together toward a solution.

Defuse the Situation

When someone comes in hot, we need to defuse the situation in order to move into healthy dialogue. Someone who is escalated needs to know they have been heard completely before any problem solving can occur. When we are clear that we are hearing what they have to say (even if we do not agree), they will often stop arguing. This is because they know we understand their point of view so they can stop explaining it. Simply saying "I hear you" or "I am making a note of that" sends the message that you are not dismissing what they have to say.

It is also important to acknowledge that the situation is of critical significance to the person in front of you. They need to understand that you are taking it seriously, and that you can see why it is so important to them. Some of our favorite sentence stems for this are:

- This is super important.
- I am so glad you brought this concern to me.
- I am taking this very seriously.
- I am so sorry this happened.

What if someone is upset about a situation because they have bad information? Maybe their child did not give an accurate picture of an incident at school, or there is a rumor circulating amongst the staff that is simply not accurate. You do not want to dismiss the concern, and you also don't want to call their child or co-worker a liar. Our go-to response in this situation is "I would be upset by that, too, if that is what I was told." This shows we are acknowledging their feelings, which are legitimate, and gives us an opening to share more information about what actually occurred.

Finally, when someone becomes dysregulated in a public space like a staff meeting, how do you diffuse the situation for everyone else? We've all been there—that one staff member says something that is shocking. Everyone looks at her for a moment, but within seconds they look to the leader to see how they are going to respond. Some staff might be wishing they had popcorn so they could binge-watch this show all day! So, what do you say? Try, "Well . . . that was unexpected." The trick to this is saying it calmly and then just moving along. This sends the message that you are calm, cool, and collected even if you have no idea how you are going to handle the situation. It also buys you a little time to make a plan. Additionally, it shows you have everything under control, instead of allowing them to derail your meeting.

Buy Time to Plan

How often do you get asked, "Hey, do you have a minute?" We are going to guess, all the time. The sad truth is: No, you do not have a minute. In fact, you have negative minutes and are already fifteen minutes late for your next appointment. Of course, if we actually say that to people, they won't hear that we are too busy. They will hear that we are too busy *for them.* It sends the message that we don't think their concern is important, or they aren't a priority, or their needs are not significant enough for us to address. We know that's not the message you are intending to send, but it is often the one that is received. Try responding with, "You are worth so much more than a minute. Let's schedule a time when we can give this the attention it deserves." Then, schedule a time that works.

There is no question that when we are able to plan for a conversation, it will go better. If someone unexpectedly comes to you with an important issue, whenever possible, move the conversation to a time that will allow you to make a plan. This is especially critical when someone is escalated. They may not know it, but they need time to cool off so the conversation can be more productive. Buying time also gives you the opportunity to do whatever preparation is necessary. You may need to do some investigating, check your thinking with trusted colleagues, or map out the conversation. Here are some sentence stems that can be extremely helpful in buying time:

- This conversation is really important. I want to make sure I can give it the time it deserves.
- I am committed to figuring out how we got here. I need some time to do some investigation so I have all the information we need to problem solve.
- This is too critical to be rushed. Let's schedule a time when we can problem-solve together.

This goes without saying, but we will say it anyway. If you use these sentence stems, you need to actually follow up as promised and make sure it gets on your schedule. If at all possible, pull out your calendar in the moment and find a time that will work for both of you. This moves the focus to scheduling versus the issue, and it shows the other person you are not just trying to put off the conversation.

CTC TIP: Don't answer your phone! This is not nearly as sneaky as it sounds. Utilize your voicemail, and enlist the help of your office staff to take a message. This ensures you can do any homework you need before returning the call. It also gives the caller a chance to cool off if they are hot. The issue is very rarely urgent, so take a beat before returning the call, unless it is an immediate safety concern. We cannot tell you how many times we've heard from people, "Oh! You are so glad you didn't answer my call this morning. I was ticked!" What we don't say is, "Yep. That's why I didn't call you back right away."

Identify a Common Purpose

In education, we are almost always on the same side. We all want what is best for kids. The disagreement is more often in determining what *best* actually is. So, it is helpful to make the common purpose explicit. When a caregiver is upset about how the school is responding to their child, it is important to show you are on the same team. It might sound like, "We both want your child to [be successful, be safe at school, learn to read, have friends, etc.] . . . let's see how we can work together to make this happen." Again, educators are also on the side of kids. So we need to point this common purpose out. Saying, "We both want your classroom to feel safe" or "I know how important it is to both of us that your students make improvements in their reading."

We all have a common purpose in education, no matter what role we hold. Taking a moment to identify those common interests, and then thinking about strategies that can work for both parties puts us on the same team. Intentionally use the words "we" and "us" in the conversation as much as possible. This shows that you are invested in working together, even if they aren't yet convinced. Here are some helpful sentence stems to set us on this path:

- How can I support you with this important issue?
- What does support look like in this situation?

- How can we move forward from here?
- We both want the same thing (the student's happiness/safety/success, the class to be well managed, student behaviors to decrease, academic results to increase).
- Knowing we have the same goal, what can we do to get there in a way that will work for both of us?
- Thanks for partnering with me on this.

Connecting It

When we are faced unexpectedly with someone who is escalated, the first thing to do is check in with ourselves and make sure we are calm and in control of our emotions. The other person will likely catch some of our calm. We can diffuse the situation by intentionally listening to show that we fully understand their feelings about an issue. We also validate that the issue is genuinely important to both them and the school. Whenever possible, we want to delay an unplanned conversation with someone who is escalated to a time and place that allows us the opportunity to plan the conversation, do any investigation necessary, and with any luck, give the escalated person an opportunity to calm down themselves. In any conversation, planned or not, taking the time to point out that we have a common purpose can go a long way in moving the conversation to a solution focused mindset.

Having an escalated person show up unexpectedly gets our hearts beating a little faster than we would like. Being prepared with some sentence stems and strategies can go a long way in helping us move through the situation successfully. When the story of this conversation is told later, and trust us–it will be–these strategies help ensure that no matter what is said, you know you showed up in a way to be proud of.

Connected Takeaways

- Focus on you first. Maintain emotional composure and avoid catching the emotions of others.
- Demonstrate careful listening so that the other person knows they are understood, even if they are not agreed with.
- Get clear on the actual issue. Look for the angst under the anger.
- Validate the importance of the situation to them and us.
- Whenever possible, move an unplanned conversation into a planned conversation.
- Identify, and explicitly state, a common purpose so that you can work towards solutions that will work for both of you.

CHAPTER 9

Caregiver Conversations: Navigating the Heat

"The involvement of parents in the education of their children is of unquestionable significance."

–(Hill & Craft, 2003, Gonzalez-DeHass, Willems, & Holbein, 2005).

No matter how reasonable and rational you are, if you have children, you know how easy it is to leave all of your good sense at the door when it comes to your own kid. Caregivers are forced to hand over control of their child's world for a significant chunk of their day. This can be hard and scary. When a caregiver's response seems out of proportion to what we are discussing, it's helpful to remind ourselves that often what they are experiencing is a very real sense of fear and anxiety.

The amount of worry that caregivers have for their children knows no bounds, and we get it. It is their job to love and protect them. Therefore, the onus is on us to build strong and trusting relationships with the primary adults in the student's life. Regardless of whether the most important adult is their mom, dad, grandma, uncle, older sibling, or any other caregiver, these partnerships are foundational. When relationships with caregivers are strong, it helps to improve student achievement, school culture, communication and equity. Of course, building these relationships is not always easy, but it is certainly worth it.

> The onus is on us to build strong and trusting relationships with the primary adults in the student's life.

Bridging a strong partnership becomes more challenging if the caregiver did not have a good experience in school themselves. If there have been mistakes the school has made along the way, that also makes it more difficult for the caregiver to trust us. Schools are often all painted with the same brush, so it really does not matter that the caregivers' experience was thirty years ago, or that it was the *last* principal who didn't follow through on a commitment. As educators, we must show them day in and day out that we are on their child's team. With time, they will come to see that we are worthy of their trust.

Start with Care

So what do we do? We do what we always do. We start with care. Before we can truly partner with caregivers, we must make sure that they know, without question, how much we care about their child. We must share this out loud, and frequently. The more often you can work positive conversations with caregivers into your daily routine, the easier this is. It also makes those conversations that are not so positive go so much smoother.

We encourage you to leverage drop-off or pick-up for these conversations, make a few positive phone calls each week, and send home some postcards highlighting something worth sharing. The more this is embedded into your routines, the better. Sharing good news has the added benefit of bringing a lot of joy to your day.

> **Before we can truly partner with caregivers, we must make sure that they know, without question, how much we care about their child.**

CTC Tip: One of our favorite ways to ensure you send positive news home for every student in a school or classroom is to print out address labels for your school, and send home positive postcards until every label has been used. Then, start again. This is super quick and easy to do. This can be done school-wide as a part of every staff meeting. It can also be done by an individual teacher or class.

Another strategy we love is to "Drop Everything and Call." As busy as we all are, we can probably find fifteen minutes in the week for our entire staff to make as many positive calls as they can during that block of time. This could be before or after school, or in place of a staff meeting. The number of smiles the next day will make it worth it–plus it is as uplifting to make these calls as it is to receive them. Be careful to have a system to ensure the same kids are not always getting a call while others never do. A more flexible way to do this is to set the expectation that everyone will make three calls each week. Again, set up a way to track it so no student gets missed. Don't forget—leaders go first. Actively modeling this and participating alongside the other educators will demonstrate that you value building a culture of connection with families.

The best and most critical way to show care? Share with them the information they need to know. As we discussed in a previous chapter, we must share news with caregivers consistently and often, even when that news is hard. In our experience, not sharing important information is almost always a mistake. When they learn you withheld details (and they almost always do), you'll have lost trust for not sharing it sooner.

Mind Your Eduspeak

We have yet to come across a profession that loves their acronyms more than education. We also seem to use a lot of terms that non-educators have never heard of. Erika and Tiffany like to refer to these as AFA or **A**nother . . . **F**antastic **A**cronym. As challenging as it may be, we urge you to work on avoiding eduspeak as much as possible when conversing with caregivers. If you do use a technical term or acronym, be sure to define it for the caregiver.

Years ago, Erika and her husband were in a meeting for her son back when he was in kindergarten and receiving articulation services. Erika knew everyone on the team because they worked together, and was also very familiar with the process, given she was a special education teacher for years. What both Erika and the team forgot is that this was all new for her husband. He confessed later that it felt like the whole meeting happened in a different language. Thankfully, Erika was able to go back through the information with him, but most folks don't have an education translator available.

When caregivers do not understand what is happening, or feel forced to ask a lot of clarifying questions, it can put them on the defensive, and make them less likely to want to partner. So mind your eduspeak. In a team meeting, it can be helpful to put one person in charge of listening for it and providing clarification.

Supporting Teachers

As you have likely seen, some teachers can be a bit reticent to initiate contact with caregivers. This could be due to a bad experience in the past, a lack of confidence, or they simply don't feel they have the time. And yet, we know that strong communication between the classroom teacher and the caregiver is crucial. It is important to remind teachers (and ourselves) if we don't invest the time now, we will be spending much more time later. Whenever possible, we recommend picking up the phone, instead of trying to share challenging information via email. We cannot tell you the number of hours we have spent on communication clean-up because someone sent an email that should have been a phone call.

We encourage you to set consistent communication with caregivers as an expectation for teachers. Clarify this expectation and then reinforce it. When a teacher brings a student issue to your attention, respond first by asking, "How did the conversation with the family go?" Unless there has been a major incident that requires an administrator, teachers should be the ones to share about something going on with a child at school.

As administrators who are pretty skilled at communication, we found that many teachers we have worked with wanted us to make all the phone calls. We are such service-oriented leaders that we needed to remind ourselves that this was not the most effective way to handle caregiver communication for a number of reasons. First, the person who is having the conversation is in the best position to build a stronger connection. The most important relationship is between the caregiver and the teacher, not the administrator. Second, the teacher is most knowledgeable about what is going on. Most often, there is no reason for us to be a go-between. Additionally, if the principal calls home for small issues, we lessen the impact when we have to make a call for big issues. Finally, if the principal is making all the phone calls, they would have little time for anything else.

When setting the expectation that teachers communicate both positive and challenging information with caregivers, provide them with the support they need. We recommend sharing this outline for caregiver conversations that we introduced in our first book. We found that this framework helps reduce some of the stress around sharing hard news. There are five basic steps:

1. Start with care
2. What happened (or is happening)
3. Why you think it happened (or is happening)
4. What happens next
5. Show care

Here is an example of how it might sound when sharing a behavioral incident:

Show care	Hi Tom, this is Nancy, Julie's math teacher. This is not an emergency, Julie is fine. I just need to share something with you that happened at school today. First, I hope you know how much I appreciate Julie and all the humor and joy she brings to our class.
What happened	Today during math class, Julie had another student's assignment on her desk, and was copying their work onto her assignment.
Why you think it happened	I've noticed that Julie has been extremely busy the last few weeks with volleyball practice, and has missed several classes because of the need to travel to away games. I'm guessing that she is probably feeling behind and overwhelmed, and wasn't sure how to do the assignment, because she missed that instruction.

What happens next	Tomorrow, and for the next three days, Julie is going to come to our classroom to serve lunch detention. We will use that time to review the concepts and work on catching up on her assignments. Because this is against the code of conduct she signed off on for athletics, she will be explaining what happened to the coach first thing in the morning–with my support. This violation typically results in sitting out at least one game.
Show care	When Julie and I spoke about this, it was clear she regrets her actions. I am confident that we will be able to navigate this together. Do you have any questions for me?

The same basic outline can be used if a teacher is noticing some academic concerns. That might sound more like this:

Show care	Hello Ms. Jackson. I am such a huge fan of Sammy. She is such a kind friend, and works so hard in class.
What happened (or is happening)	I have been noticing that Sammy is struggling with reading. Again, she is working really hard, however she is having a hard time sounding out more complex words.
Why you think it happened (or is happening)	I think part of the struggle is that she is working in the large classroom group and we are not explicitly teaching how to sound out these words as a whole class.
What happens next	We have a block of time each morning that we call "WIN" time, which stands for **W**hat **I N**eed. During this time, I would like Sammy to begin working with our reading specialist in a small group so they can really focus on these skills. I feel Sammy will have more success with this skill once she is able to learn it in a smaller group setting.
Show care	Sammy works so hard, and is so determined to become a fluent reader. I am so proud of her effort, as I am sure you are. She brings such a light to our class. Can I answer any questions for you?

Depending on the teacher's level of comfort and experience, consider helping them prepare for this in advance (We created a template for you to use as a free resource on our website www.connectingthroughconversation.com and in the appendix of this book). You may even offer to sit with them while they make the call, if they are particularly worried. Just having you present is sometimes all they need to feel confident and supported. The key thing is *they* are making the call. The more they do it, the more comfortable they will become and the more our culture of connection will grow. Plus, the more you build capacity with the staff around communication, the more time you'll have.

When It's the Administrator's Call

No matter how successful you are in building the capacity of teachers in your building to make these calls, there will be times that it really is your call to make. This should be reserved for those incidents that result in a significant consequence, when previous attempts by the teacher regarding a pattern of behavior were unsuccessful, or when student safety is involved. When it is up to you, utilize the same five steps we outlined above:

1. Start with Care
2. What happened (or is happening)
3. Why you think it happened (or is happening)
4. What happens next

A few tips when you have to share hard behavioral information with a caregiver. First, if at all possible, make sure the caregiver has the information before the student leaves for the day. This allows you to frame the situation for the caregiver instead of the student. Also, remember that getting a call from an administrator at your child's school can be scary, especially if teachers are making the majority of these calls. So, don't dive in until you have assured them that their child is physically okay.

> **CTC Tip:** When it makes sense, have the student share with the caregiver, in your presence, what happened. By calling them on speaker phone you do a couple of things. First, it increases the accountability for that student. Second, the caregiver is far less likely to argue that their child could never do such a thing. If you choose this approach it is important to coach the student on what information must be included, how to take accountability, and that they must be honest. Once they have given their caregiver the basic information, you can share any next steps or needed follow up.

If you are sharing a consequence for the student, it is important to share how this is meant to help the student learn. After all, the goal of the consequence is to change the behavior so they don't make the same mistake again in the future. Always end the conversation with a reminder that you care about their child, and thank them for teaming with you to support the student through the situation.

Common Caregiver Stumbling Blocks

As we said at the start of this chapter, even the most calm, reasonable, rationale among us can respond in the exact opposite way when it comes to our child. We get it. It is sometimes hard to admit our child has made a mistake. When our child has made a mistake, it can also make us feel embarrassed, question our parenting, or put us on the defensive. These patterns can play out in some predictable ways. We would like to reshare what we call Common Caregiver Stumbling Blocks from *Connecting Through Conversation: A Playbook for Talking with Students* (Bare & Burns, 2023, pp.146-148).

Common Caregiver Stumbling Blocks

- **What about the other kid?** Caregivers are often concerned that any consequence their student is getting is the same as another student involved, regardless of different circumstances. A Connected Communicator's response is to share that we can't talk about another student, in the same way we would never disclose information about their child. You may also have to explain that fair is not always equal, and in the same way we are considering the uniqueness of their student and what they need, we are doing the same for any other student involved. While being careful not to be too specific, we can share what typical consequences or action steps might be when students demonstrate similar types of behaviors.
- **My kid would never!** This, of course, is a favorite. If you are a parent, you know we are often struck blind out of love for our child. It is also hard to not be embarrassed or feel that it is a statement on your parenting if your child does something you are not proud of at

school. Denial is the easiest course for that caregiver to take. The best offense in this situation is to have the student be the one to share what they did. It is unlikely that the parent is going to call their own child a liar. It may also be useful to say something like, "I can understand why this is so hard to wrap your head around. This seems out of character for Oliver. Nevertheless, he did make this unexpected choice this time. My concern now is partnering together to support him in assuring it does not happen again."

- **You can't do this!** Be prepared to share school and board policy at this point. Have your school handbook handy. This is the time to share both the rationale, and how you are supported by policy. Offer to share a copy with them.

- **I'm going to your boss.** Connected Communicators have fostered relationships of trust with their boss. When caregivers let us know that they intend to go to the principal, superintendent, School Board etc. there is no need for us to worry. We have followed policy, and have done our best job in a challenging situation. To the caregiver, simply offer to share the contact information of the appropriate person or the complaint process with them. When they see that you are not concerned that they are taking it to the next person, they are less likely to follow through because they know you are confident in your actions. Always give the person they will be going to a heads up that someone may be coming their way along with your version of what took place. We never want to surprise our boss.

Maintain Boundaries

Partnering with caregivers is a priority, and yet so is maintaining boundaries. These boundaries help ensure that our communication is healthy and, ideally, harmonious.

Speak respectfully: We can completely understand why caregivers might lose their cool a bit when it comes to their child. However, understanding where they are coming from does not mean we are obligated to take abuse. We know it can be quite stressful, but if you are talking to a caregiver who is using profanity, yelling, and utilizing personal attacks, it is imperative to end the conversation.

Of course, this is much easier to say than to do. There is no comfortable way to do this, and it is difficult to do gracefully. So, what does it look like? The first time the caregiver says something inappropriate, provide a warning. That might be, "That is not respectful language. I will not talk to or about you in that way. I insist you show me and my fellow educators the same respect." Let them know you will be ending the conversation if it happens again. If it does happen again, say something like, "It is clear that we are unable to have this conversation in a respectful way. We are going to end our conversation for today, and I will be in touch to schedule a follow-up time when we can be more productive."

When you are talking to someone who is simply too elevated to be productive, we also have to end the conversation. We recommend acknowledging how upset they are, and then rescheduling for a later time. For example:

- "I can tell you are upset, and that makes sense. We will be able to have a more productive conversation after we have both taken some time. I will contact you to schedule a time to complete our conversation."

- "I can hear that you are angry and I can understand why you might feel that way. It is hard for me to hear you when you are yelling. Let's try to have this conversation again when we are both a little calmer." *As a warning, do not tell them to calm down. Tiffany will never forget the time she told a parent that they needed to be calm in order for them to continue the conversation and the parent yelled, very loudly, "I AM CALM!"*

If the parent refuses to end the call or meeting and continues with inappropriate behavior, you must take the next step. If you have warned them, offered to reschedule, and they continue, it's time to end the conversation. Say either, "I am hanging up now" or "I am leaving the meeting now" and then do it. This becomes all the more important when you are in a meeting with other staff members. They need to know that you have their back and will not allow them to be verbally attacked. As the leader in the meeting, everyone is looking to you to handle it if things go sideways. If you don't end the meeting, it's very likely that the staff members will first be upset with the caregiver. However, later, it's just as likely that they will be upset with you for allowing it to continue.

When a conversation must come to an end because of inappropriate behavior, it is important to get back in touch. You'll want to give things some time to cool off before attempting to reengage. When you do, we recommend you establish some ground rules for communication, and ensure that you do not meet with them alone. Be clear on what communication needs to look like, and then maintain that expectation.

Send a reasonable amount of communication via email: You may find yourself in a situation where a parent's communication verges on harassment due to the sheer quantity of communication. They are emailing several times a day and demanding an immediate response. And then when you do respond, it's met with three more emails. In a case like this, we recommend advising the parent that you will be responding only twice a week, regardless of how many emails they send. Keep your responses brief and *only answer direct questions.* If it is just a series of complaints, think about whether it's even necessary to respond. If it is necessary, you may want to simply respond with, "I am sorry you feel that way." Do not get into a back-and-forth via email, stick to answering the direct questions only.

The idea that we only respond to direct questions does not just apply to email. It is also a helpful strategy when meeting with someone. Tiffany remembers a time early in her administrative career when she was working with a parent who made it clear that he was unwilling to work toward solutions and only focused on personal attacks. One day, he came into her office and shared a lengthy litany of complaints, most of which were either untrue, or had been addressed previously. When the parent was finished, Tiffany thanked him for the feedback, stood up, and walked to the door to escort him out. The parent looked bewildered and loudly sputtered, "Well, don't you have anything you want to say for yourself?!" Tiffany responded, "No. I didn't hear you ask any questions. But I do appreciate the feedback. Thank you." She then escorted him out. He wasn't happy, but he did stop barraging her with complaints.

If a caregiver is communicating in that same way with a staff member, as the administrator, you'll need to set that boundary. Let the caregiver know that the staff member is busy doing their job, and is unable to respond to this quantity of emails. Depending on the tenor of the emails, tell them to either direct future communications to you, or you can advise them that the staff member will only be responding once or twice a week on a set day.

> **CTC Tip:** In these situations, be kind to yourself and make sure you are centered *before* reading those emails. Maybe you will take some deep breaths before opening. Or plan to go for a short walk afterwards. Be sure to avoid reading emails from this person outside of work hours. We cannot tell you how many weekends have been ruined because we read a nasty-gram on a Saturday morning. Learn from our mistakes, and take care of yourself—and your staff.

Caregivers Need to Come to Agreement on Their Own Time: When we have two caregivers who live in different house-holds and are on very different pages, we often find ourselves stuck in the middle. Unless directed by the courts through a custody agreement or court order, we communicate with both caregivers equally. It will help us tremendously to establish a communication protocol in advance. We recommend com-municating to them both at the same time whenever possible, and to tell them that you will be communicating in this way. When two caregivers cannot be in the same room together, offer to have one on the phone and the other in person, or make it an entirely virtual meeting. Ensure both caregivers are included in all written communication. If one emails you, cc the other on your response. If there is a phone call with one, a summary of conversation should be sent afterwards to both parties.

When there are disagreements, and there very likely will be, we advise that you ask them to discuss on their own and then let us know what they decide to do. It can be tempting to just go to the caregiver that we agree with on any given issue. This can get us into trouble, and cause such a headache down the road. Tiffany will forever remember when the school team recommended a special education evaluation to a family during a meeting with both parents. The mom left early and the dad gave consent. Later that afternoon, the mom came in and revoked consent. The next day the dad came in and gave a new consent. There was no custody agreement on file so it was quite the circus until they got it sorted. If Tiffany could go back in time, she would have let both parents know that they need to get on the same page, and then let the school know how they would both like to proceed.

Connecting It

Our students are better off when we partner closely with their caregivers. To do this, we need to communicate with them often and with care. Make sure they know how much we love their kid, and that we are on the same team. Set the expectation with staff that we are going to communicate with caregivers, even when it is hard. Caregivers can lose their ability to be rational when it comes to their own children. We have seen this lead to some patterns that we call common caregiver stumbling blocks. Be ready for them so you know how to work around them. It is critical that we also hold boundaries with caregivers. We must insist that they speak to and about educators respectfully, and do not yell or make personal attacks. Additionally, we will not respond to a communication avalanche or be the go-between when there are two caregivers on very different pages. Remember, we are on the caregivers' team because we are all working together for the best possible things for their child.

Connected Takeaways

- Children are better off when we have strong partnerships with their caregivers.
- Share good news with caregivers as often as possible.
- Use the communication outline when contacting caregivers about something difficult:
- Maintain boundaries, speak respectfully, send a reasonable amount of information via email, come to agreement on your own time.

CHAPTER 10

Planning for a Heated Conversation

"It takes as much energy to wish as it does to plan."

–Eleanor Roosevelt

Once we realize that we need to have a tough conversation, we typically start to feel a bit anxious–after all, the stakes are high. We have found the best antidote to anxiety is action. For us, this action involves making a plan, and taking the first step is often the hardest part. We like to use the planning guide you will find in our appendix to help get started. By getting our thoughts down on paper, and then carefully considering each step, we feel prepared and ready. This allows us to enter tough conversations with clarity and confidence. And, by thinking it through carefully in advance, there is a much higher chance it will go smoothly.

> The best antidote to anxiety is action.

Purpose

We now know all tough conversations need to be grounded in care. So, the first step in planning is to make sure that is the case. Get crystal clear on the purpose of the conversation, and ensure your motivation is that you care about the person, the students, or the relationship. It might sound like this:

- Ms. Wheeler needs support with behavior management on her bus route, and I care about their safety.
- I care about Sam's success, and the school needs to reestablish trust with his dad in order for us to partner together to help Sam at school.
- Mr. Bleak's attitude is having a negative impact on the school culture. He seems very unhappy, and I care about him and the impact he is having on our students and staff.

One of the reasons we ground ourselves in care as we start planning the conversation is to assess our own motivations. If our purpose is grounded in anything other than care, it would be wise to pause. If we find ourselves wanting to put a teacher in their place, or prove a point with a parent—STOP. This is such an easy trap to fall into. Let's imagine we have a paraprofessional, Mr. Brazen, who stands up in a staff meeting and says something truly outrageous. Our recommended response would be to say, "Well . . . that was unexpected. Mr. Brazen, I'll follow up with you on that later." Now, you've bought yourself some time, but you will have to follow up. For some of us, the motivation might initially be to sit them down in our office and give them a piece of our mind. We get it, but telling someone off is not grounded in care for anything but our own ego. That does not mean we do not need to schedule that important conversation. But it does mean we need to wait until our motivation is rooted in care.

OK, now that we know we are entering into the conversation based on care, we ask ourselves the following questions we learned from *Crucial Conversations* by Patterson, Renny, McMillan and Switzler.

1. What do I want out of this conversation?
2. What do I want the other person to gain from this conversation?
3. What do I want for our relationship?

By focusing on these questions, it ensures we stay on track as we map out the conversation. With Mr. Brazen, the answers might sound like this:

- What do I want out of this conversation?
  I want to be assured that a similar situation will not reoccur in the staff meeting. I want to keep the culture of our school professional and focused on learning for both the students and the staff. I want to ensure we always speak about our students in a respectful manner.

- What do I want the other person to gain from this conversation?
  I want Mr. Brazen to know the impact he has on staff and our culture when he acts unprofessionally in meetings. I want him to share his frustrations in a way that will allow for problem solving. I want him to act

and speak with restraint and consider his word choice before speaking in a public setting.

- What do I want for our relationship?
  I want to build trust between Mr. Brazen and myself. It is important to me that he trusts me enough to come to me directly with his concerns in the future and that I can trust him to get his concerns addressed in a professional manner.

Method

Once we have clearly identified the purpose of the conversation, we need to choose a method of communicating. It may not seem like an important step, but we have lost count of the number of times we've had to do communication clean-up because the method chosen wasn't compatible with the message.

When there is nuanced information to communicate, it should not be done electronically. Email communicates one-way information. It is not useful for dialog or an exchange of ideas. Email also doesn't transmit tone, nor does it allow you to see how the message has landed. So, although it may feel like sending an email is a quick and easy way to get the message out, an email that should have been a conversation will cost you more in the end.

Email is, however, a great tool for sharing information that needs to be documented or referred to afterwards. In a later chapter, we discuss how to follow up a tough conversation with a summary-of-conversation email to ensure everyone remembers what was agreed to or discussed.

There are a number of apps now available for home-to-school communication that can be super useful. However, if ever you need to share with a caregiver something significant, we strongly caution you from sending that information via an app. Instead, pick up the phone or set up a meeting. Tiffany vividly remembers a time that a caregiver showed up absolutely livid because her child had been hurt during an altercation at recess and she learned about it from her child's teacher in an app.

The Invitation

After considering the various methods of communication, it is clear that we need to schedule a sit-down meeting. That means we send an invitation. It may feel like an easy step, and yet it is actually quite nuanced. First, you must consider *when* to send the invitation. You want to ensure that those you are inviting have enough time to prepare, and yet we don't want them to spend so much time between the invitation and the meeting that their anxiety gets out of control. With too much time, they often make up a story in their head that is not at all true or helpful. Or they turn into a town crier and attempt to rally their co-workers. So, we recommend providing 24 to 48 hours' notice for a meeting related to staff performance.

Sending the invitation late on a Friday afternoon is likely to cause anxiety and frustration. We know there are times when making someone uncomfortable is the strategy. We urge you to only employ this when absolutely necessary or in extreme circumstances, as we discuss in detail in the chapter *Putting Coaching Out into Action.*

Recently, an administrator told us about a time they were rushing to get out the door for the weekend and knew they needed to meet with a teacher on Monday to discuss a low-level concern that a parent had brought them that afternoon. In their rush, they sent an invitation to that teacher on Friday at 4:45 p.m. without including any details. The invitation was titled "Parent Complaint." The administrator had a strict rule about not responding to emails over the weekend, so the teacher's requests for more information went unanswered. The teacher spent all weekend racking her brain about what and who it could be about. She also called many of her colleagues and worked herself into a frenzy. When they finally met, the teacher was so anxious and escalated that the conversation became about the invitation, and not the parent complaint. To make matters worse, the teacher shared this story with her colleagues, which caused damage to the administrator's relationships with multiple members of the staff.

So, how much information do you include in the invitation? We strive for the Goldie Locks approach here. We want to share enough information that they know what the topic is, but not so much information that you end up holding the meeting before the meeting. In the example above, if the administrator had only included the student's name and given a concise description of the nature of the complaint, the teacher would not have spent the weekend trying to figure out what it was all about. Most often, they will tell themselves a story that is far worse than what actually needs to be discussed, so save you both the headache and share just enough.

We also want to make sure the appropriate people are included in the invite. If we are meeting with caregivers, make sure to include any primary caregivers (don't invite one, and forget the other, especially if they are not in the same household). If there is likely going to be discipline for a staff member as a result of the meeting, advise them to bring a union representative, and don't forget to alert your HR director.

If you know a staff member is bringing their union representative, the union president, and their grade level partner, you might have someone there for you to help balance the scales a bit. Invite someone from your Human Resources department, or another administrator if you have a team at your school. They can take notes, and help keep others on track. Even when you are in charge, it can be helpful and supportive to have an ally next to you.

Timing

When should the meeting be scheduled? With staff, schedule it at a time that is going to have the least impact on their ability to get back to work. If it is likely the teacher will be too impacted by the conversation to return to their classroom right away, schedule the meeting for the end of the day. If the educator is going to be too unsettled to focus on their work until the conversation has taken place, schedule it first thing in the morning. If you know the staff member is going to retell the conversation to anyone who will listen and that's unhelpful, consider scheduling the meeting for the very end of the day or before a weekend. For caregivers, we want to make it as convenient for them as possible, while not asking our staff to work outside of their contract hours.

We know your calendar is full–you're an educator! It can be easy to underestimate the amount of time a meeting is going to take, especially when we are trying to sandwich it into an already-packed day. Before you send an invite for twenty minutes, remind yourself it is likely to be hugely impactful for the educator or caregiver. So, schedule enough time to ensure the conversation is not rushed. When you are in the middle of an important conversation, you don't want the added pressure of not having enough time.

> **CTC Tip:** Schedule fifteen minutes more than you think you will need for a meeting. If the meeting finishes at the time you anticipated, you now have a luxurious fifteen extra minutes. These meetings can take a lot out of us. Having a few minutes after the meeting to capture the notes, recoup, or take a quick walk can be extremely useful.

The Location

Where should the meeting take place? Well, that depends. If you want the other person to be as comfortable as possible, go to their space. If it requires privacy and a bit more gravity, hold the conversation in your office. If the conversation is serious, and involves multiple people, use the conference room.

Oftentimes, when we meet with a staff member and their union representative, they need time after the meeting to discuss. This is awkward if you begin the meeting in your office. It's uncomfortable to ask a visibly upset staff member to find another place to meet. If you leave them in your office, you won't have access to anything you might need until they are done. Or worse—you have to keep interrupting to grab your keys, walkie, cell, etc. That is why we recommend holding those meetings in the conference room. Then you can leave and offer them the space.

In the case of Mr. Brazen, since it's the first time anything like this has occurred, it will likely not be disciplinary assuming it does not recur. It is important that we have privacy for the conversation, and that he understands that it is being taken seriously. For all these reasons, we would select our office for the conversation.

When thinking about location, you also want to consider the seating arrangements. Your seat should have direct access to the exit, have a view of a clock, and if possible, allow you to make eye contact with someone in the office. With Mr. Brazen, we would sit in our favorite spot at the round table in our office. This allows us to sit at an angle to him with a view of the door and the clock.

Whenever possible, sit next to the person you are meeting with, or at ninety degrees. As we discuss in the chapter *Body Position Matters Too*, this allows us to be in a non-confrontational stance, does not demand eye contact, and allows us to easily use the third point. Sitting near the door and with a view of someone in the office is important if there is a chance the meeting could go so sideways that you need to end the meeting (more on this later). In that case, you want to be able to reach the door without needing to squeeze by someone else. Having a view of the clock allows you to ensure you are on track with time without rudely checking your watch or phone.

> **CTC Tip:** When we are holding a meeting with multiple people, we like to claim our seat first. We leave our blank note pad and water by the seat we want well before the start time of the meeting.

What Needs to be Communicated

Part of the preparation is making sure that you have done your homework, and have all the information needed for the conversation. We recommend that you write any important information down on the planning guide so that you can refer to it during the meeting. Remember to keep your notes objective, and stick to the facts. Be as specific as possible. If you have discussed this issue with them previously, have the details of those conversations in front of you. When providing feedback on behaviors, have the dates, times, locations, and circumstances at your fingertips.

Gather any artifacts or evidence needed to support the conversation. This could be data from an observation, email exchanges, notes from phone conversations, written complaints, etc. With families, this could include academic data, attendance or behavior records, and so on. Utilizing the third point shifts the emotional energy away from the people and onto the data.

When discussing a classroom observation with a teacher, take a close look to ensure that it has been recorded objectively. When conducting an observation, we should only record things we can observe—what the teacher did or said, what the students did or said, or what is in the environment. There are many books on taking objective classroom observation data, so we won't get into that here, but if you want to learn more, we recommend *Learning Focused Conversations (2018)* by Laura Lipton and Bruce Wellman.

You'll also want to write down the things that have to be said, especially those things that you know are going to be difficult for you to say. This accomplishes a few things. First, it can be used as a starting point for the notes you take during the meeting. It also holds you accountable and ensures you don't wiggle out of saying the hard thing. After all, if you wrote it down, you know you need to say it. Finally, it ensures we do not forget to share a critical piece of information. Having this prepared ahead of time makes something really hard just a little bit easier.

CTC Tip: Tiffany likes to take these notes in light pencil on her yellow pad. This allows her to have access to her notes, but the other person will not be able to read what it says.

When preparing to speak with Mr. Brazen, we would make note of the following:

- In the staff meeting on Tuesday, while we were discussing various ways to gather and use formative assessment data, you said in a voice that everyone could hear, "All this trendy nonsense about formative whatever is a waste of time. We need to be talking about how to enforce the dress code. Girls are showing up to school dressed like hussies."
- Four staff members came to me after the meeting and indicated that the comment was both off topic

and unprofessional. They expressed that referring to students in this way was disparaging and not in alignment with our stated value of speaking about our students with respect and kindness.
- This comment was disruptive, off topic, and displayed a lack of professionalism that is not acceptable.
- One of our meeting agreements is we will stick to the agenda and use a parking lot for items not on the agenda.

Anticipating Obstacles

As part of the planning process, it is helpful to try and anticipate some of the obstacles or challenges that may come up in the conversation. For example, if you are going to be meeting with a parent regarding their child's behavior, and you have already acknowledged that there was a situation at the start of the year that was not handled well by the teacher, it is wise to anticipate that this is likely to come up again. Make a plan in advance to acknowledge this so the team can move forward. If you know you are sitting down with someone who often has a hard time staying on track, prepare an agenda to keep everyone on topic.

Although we are not engaging in a debate, it can be helpful to prepare a response to any arguments that you can anticipate. For example, if you are sitting down with a teacher who has an unusually large class this year, be proactive in thinking about the supports you might put in place to address the class size issue. This allows you to focus on the actual issue at hand. Although it is not possible to anticipate every challenge that may arise, spending some time thinking proactively can go a long way to making the conversation go to plan.

Connecting It

When we need to have a tough conversation, a little bit of planning can make a big difference. We encourage you to use the planning guide provided in the Appendix to guide you through the process. As part of the preparation, get clear on your motivation for having the conversation and ensure it is based in care. Consider carefully the location you want the conversation to take place, and the timing of both the meeting and the invitation. Do your homework and gather all of the information that needs to be shared and either write it down, or bring a physical copy of items that are being discussed. By taking these steps in advance, you will feel more prepared and comfortable engaging in the conversation, and hopefully sleep a bit easier the night before.

> When we need to have a tough conversation, a little bit of planning can make a big difference.

Connected Takeaways

- The purpose of the conversation must be rooted in care.
- Get clear on your answers to the following questions:
    - What do I want out of this conversation?
    - What do I want the other person to gain from this conversation?
    - What do I want for our relationship?
- Send an invitation 24 - 48 hours in advance of the meeting for staff. Use the Goldie Locks approach and share just enough.

- Prepare what needs to be communicated and gather artifacts and evidence.
- Anticipate obstacles that may come up, and make a plan to address them.

CHAPTER 11

Keeping Things Cool in the Conversation

"Learning that you can't control the other person's reaction, and that it can be destructive to try, can be incredibly liberating."

—Douglas Stone, Bruce Patton, and Shelia Heen, *Difficult Conversations: How to Discuss What Matters Most* (1999, p. 152)

It's time for the conversation. You are prepared. You have made sure you are in the correct headspace, you are clear on your motivation, and you have done your homework. You are ready, and you've got this. Now you just need to keep the conversation going in the right direction. As the proverbial train starts moving, it is our job to help keep it on track. This is simply not as easy as we would like it to be. Here are a few tips to help keep things headed to your desired destination.

Identify the Logic

When we are in a conversation that requires us to bring someone alongside, or agree to do something differently, we need to use our powers of persuasion. This is when it is helpful to remember that there are two types of logic people respond to when making decisions. One is a logic based on data and reasoning and another is a logic based on empathy and feeling. Charles Duhigg explains this well in his book, *Supercommunicators: How to Unlock the Secret Language of Connection* (2024).

When we find ourselves needing to persuade someone else, it is extremely helpful to spend time thinking about which type of logic will be most effective. Is this person going to be convinced by data and reasoning? If so, we are bringing hard facts to the table, sharing the research, and pointing out the logical reasons this is the best way forward. Or, on the other hand, is this person going to be persuaded by a more empathetic approach? If the latter is the case, we are going to lean into the story. We are going to share a scenario or offer a narrative account of the personal impact on others.

All of us can be influenced by both types of logic, depending on the type of situation or decision being made. At the same time, some people tend to lean more heavily in one direction than the other. So, consider the person you are talking with and what is going to be most impactful for them.

CTC Tip: When you are making a change in your organization, you will need to include logic and reasoning as well as some compelling stories in your rationale in order to convince both kinds of thinkers in your organization.

Many years ago, Erika had the challenge of ensuring equitable access to advanced coursework, specifically Advanced Placement (AP) courses. When reviewing the data, she found that the students in special education and students of color were under-represented in these courses. She was struggling to convince the department heads who made up the leadership team on campus that a change was necessary. She was in yet another conversation with the leadership team and getting nowhere fast. Erika realized that she had been using student stories to try and convince them of the need to make changes. She had not shared the data in a compelling way. These folks were going to be moved by data, not story. So, Erika pulled out the spreadsheets, showed the outcomes and demographic groups, and suddenly her job of persuading was done. Those department heads became the biggest champions for making the changes needed to address disproportionality within the AP courses.

Avoid the Kitchen Sink

Have you ever been in a conflict with someone about one thing, and suddenly every conflict that has ever occurred starts getting thrown your way? This is called "kitchen sinking." This is neither productive nor helpful. So, let's say you sit down with a teacher to discuss the importance of using the adopted language arts curriculum, and they start talking about the heater not working in their room, a "difficult" class, a conflict in their professional learning community, and the time they missed prep three weeks ago. When this happens, it is important to get things back on track. Instead of addressing each issue at that moment, redirect it or schedule it for another time. You might say, "I can see that is an important issue. We can schedule another time to address it, but today we need to stay focused on the language arts curriculum." If it is an issue that has been addressed previously, or it is not something that needs to be followed up on, then redirect. This can sound like, "Nevertheless, today we need to focus on the language arts curriculum" or "Even so, today we are talking about the language arts curriculum."

If instead of rescheduling or redirecting we start refuting every concern they bring up, we end up sounding defensive, and that simply will not help us solve the issue in front of us. Yet, responding is super tempting to do. Leaders are helpers and problem-solvers, so it's very easy for us to want to respond to issues they raise. Do your best to resist that urge. Don't provide them an opening to get you off track by addressing unrelated concerns in that moment. If you start drifting off topic, notice what's happening, pause, and redirect the conversation back to the topic at hand. Of course, if there is an issue that needs following up on, be sure to actually follow up–just not in that meeting.

Stay Focused

Now, it is equally important to avoid the temptation to start kitchen sinking them. In your preparation, you got crystal clear on what you want out of this conversation for you and for them. If you find yourself slipping down a path that is not helping you reach those goals, it is time to refocus on what you really want.

In order to stay in the right head space, we encourage you to consistently check in on your motivation. If you find yourself feeling like you need to "win" in what is becoming a battle of wills, you have gotten off track. Remind yourself of the purpose of the conversation, and the motivation you identified as you prepared.

You also want to look out for signs that you are responding out of anger. When we come from a place of anger, there is a danger that we can start to shame the other person, or attack them personally. In either case, we are shutting down both dialog and the likelihood of reaching our goals for the conversation. We must be sure that we are attacking the problem or the conflict–not the person. For example, if a teacher decided not to participate in the drill designed to support student safety, we must focus on the action, not the teacher. Saying, "Not participating in these drills puts student safety at risk" is very different from, "You don't care about student safety."

Share Your Story, Ask for Theirs

In *Crucial Conversations* (2012), the authors teach us the concept of sharing the story we are telling ourselves and then asking the other person for the story they are telling themselves. As humans we try to make meaning out of everything, often without a complete picture. Imagine that you call out to someone to say hello and they keep walking. You make up a whole story in your head about how they don't like you, and the truth is they simply didn't hear you. We do this all the time when ascribing motivations to people, or trying to imagine why something took place. We also tend to put ourselves at the center of the story, even though it likely has little to do with us. So, whenever possible, identify when you are telling yourself a story. Is this grounded in fact, or is it an interpretation? If it is a story, bring it to the other person and ask them to share what is actually going on.

For example, let's imagine that you have emailed a teacher three reminders to complete their goal setting for the year. This is a required part of the evaluation process. You start to tell yourself a story that the teacher does not take you seriously, and that when you share with them an expectation, they see it as a suggestion. You are also wondering if they think they don't have to follow the required process because they have been a successful teacher for a number of years.

First, **share the actual facts**. That might sound like, "I have not yet received your goals for the year. I have emailed you three times requesting them. They were due last Friday." This is just a retelling of what is actual, no descriptors or judgements included. When sharing the facts, we want to make sure that we are as specific as possible. Refer to documents, dates, times, and emails as much as possible. Be careful to avoid always and never statements. There should be no way to dispute or argue this part of the conversation–it is all just data.

Then **tell your story.** It is important here to state that it is a story you are telling yourself, not facts. You can even temper it if what you think is especially problematic. So you could say, "I am telling myself a story that you think the goal-setting process is unnecessary for you to do given your strong track record as a teacher. It has also made me question if you are taking this directive seriously. I'm sure this isn't true, but I've even begun to wonder if you take me seriously as a supervisor."

A critical next step is to ask for their story. This is where we ask questions to help us understand how close our story is to the truth. The trick here is we must be genuinely open to their answer. Remember, there is a chance, even a good chance, our story is entirely fiction. In this example we could ask, "Can you tell me what is really going on?" or "Can you help me understand what is getting in the way of completing this?" or simply, "Is that right?"

When presenting a story that may or may not be true, the authors of *Crucial Conversations* caution us to talk tentatively. You will notice instead of saying, "You don't take me seriously" it was softened considerably by saying, "I've even begun to wonder if . . . "There are a number of qualifiers that can support dialogue as opposed to putting someone on the defensive. For example:

- I am beginning to wonder . . .
- I'm starting to think . . .
- In my opinion . . .
- My perception is . . .
- Perhaps you were unaware of . . .

All these qualifiers make it clear that you are presenting your story, and you are open to more information to help set the record straight.

Finding the Common Ground

In education, we all have a similar purpose. If you examine your school's mission statement, it likely has an element of preparing students for their future, fostering a safe and supportive learning environment, supporting academic excellence, and educating the whole child. You will be hard-pressed to find an educator who does not want those things for their students.

This makes the common ground easy to find with educators. We just need to point it out. Something like, "I know we both want [our students to achieve academic excellence, to feel safe, to feel cared for, etc.]" As we've stated previously, the disagreement is typically not in *what* we want, but in *how* we get there. Of course the same is true with caregivers. Both the caregiver and the educator want what is best for the student. We may just disagree on what that best thing is. Although the common ground is right there, it is most often not obvious to the other person. In a difficult conversation, the person we are talking with isn't typically thinking, "Wow. We have so much in common. We both want the same thing for this student." Since they aren't thinking about it, we need to say it. Explicitly.

If you find yourself at an impasse, look for the way forward that will work for both of you. For example, let's imagine that a caregiver is arguing that their child needs to have a one-on-one assistant with them for the entirety of the school day. The educators are concerned that this level of support is too restrictive for this student. The caregiver is concerned that without a one-on-one, the student will not be successful academically.

We recommend starting by stating the common purpose. In this case, we both want the student to be academically successful. Then, it is time to explore solutions that will work for both of us. Perhaps the student needs additional support for reading, but is otherwise independent in other academic tasks when accommodations are provided. In that case, maybe it is most helpful for an additional adult to assist during reading instruction, and look for other less-restrictive levels of support during the rest of the day.

Any time we can take a part of the solution from the other person in the conflict and combine it or change it in order for it to work for us, we are leaning into the "Genius of the AND" as opposed to the "The Tyranny of the OR" as described by Jim Collins in his book, *Built to Last* (1995). By getting away from the idea that I am right and you are wrong, we can refocus on our common purpose and find a way forward that works for all of us.

Stay Strong

Remember, you came into the conversation because you care enough to have it. Don't talk yourself out of saying the hard thing. This can happen in the heat of a difficult conversation all too easily. If you find yourself holding back in order to keep the peace or protect feelings, channel Brené Brown, who reminds us, "Clear is kind."

Another barrier to saying what we need to say is when we start taking responsibility for the emotions of the other person. It is likely that in a high-stakes conversation emotions will run high. Sometimes, the other person becomes extremely upset. When that happens, avoid back-tracking or softening your message to the point where it loses meaning. For goodness sake, don't make all the angst of this conversation be for nothing by undoing the work you have already started. Remind yourself what you really want out of the conversation, for both you and them, and persevere. We cannot be responsible for the emotions of others. We can only be responsible for how

> We cannot be responsible for the emotions of others. We can only be responsible for how we show up for the conversation.

we show up for the conversation. So, remain your best self, show empathy, but still carry on.

This is why we write down the hard things we must say in advance. By writing it down, we are committing to ourselves that we are going to say it. Somehow having it down on paper helps to hold ourselves accountable.

Connecting It

It is easy to get thrown off track once you find yourself in the middle of a heated conversation. In order to get to your destination, stay focused on what you want for you, for the other person, and for your relationship. Think about the logic style that will be the most compelling, and lean into either data or empathy. Be open in sharing the story you are telling yourself, and invite them to help set the record straight. Look for common ground, stay focused on the purpose, and don't wiggle out of saying the hard thing. You did it!

Connected Takeaways

- Throughout the conversation, stay focused on what you really want.
- Use the logic style (story or data) that will be the most effective. Avoid the kitchen sink.
- Make sure you avoid any personal attacks, blaming, or shaming.
- Share your story, and ask for theirs.
- Look for the common ground, and point it out explicitly.
- Stay strong, and say the hard things.

CHAPTER 12

Putting Out the Fire: Bringing It to a Close

*"Be clear about your message. Simplicity is
the key to effective communication."*

—Dianna Booher

You know that moment in a challenging conversation when we become painfully aware that everything that needs to be said has been said, and we are suddenly talking in circles? All the information has been shared, everyone has been listened to, and there is a plan of action (even if we don't agree on the plan). This is the time to bring the meeting to a close.

It is paramount that we maximize how we wrap these conversations up, because the last thing we hear is often what is remembered most clearly. When we bring things to a close with skill, it solidifies the expectations and path forward.

Points of Agreement

As you are wrapping up, identify points of agreement. Even if it feels super small, like agreeing that something is in violation of the handbook or what time the work day starts. We know sometimes you have to dig deep for it; say it anyway. Let's imagine we are ending the meeting with a student's parents. It might sound like, "I am so glad that we both agree that your son, Strike, hitting his teammate after practice is unacceptable and is also out of character for him. We have all noticed that there have been some shifts in mood and personality these past few months, and it is going to be important for us to work together to identify what is troubling him." When we disagree about something (especially consequences), it is very helpful that we take the time to identify points of agreement that we did have. This highlights areas where we are aligned, instead of only focusing on areas we are not.

Perhaps the point of agreement is data driven. This is important to point out because it is hard to argue. You might say, "We both agree that students are not making desired progress in this area" or "We can agree that during this observation, three of the twenty-seven students responded verbally during the ten-minute discussion." Once the problem is framed as a point of agreement, we can then move into problem solving together.

So, as you summarize the meeting, include those points of agreement, even if there is only one. It helps us wrap up on the same page and gives a place from which to build. Additionally, pointing out where we agree helps to overcome negativity bias, or the tendency to pay more attention to disagreement or tension. People are not generally wired to pay attention to the positive, so help them remember it and frame it as a take-away. It can also give us some often much-needed common ground to move forward.

Clarify Next Steps

Before you go your separate ways, it is critical to be clear on the next steps so that everyone knows what to expect following the meeting. Succinctly and explicitly listing these out loud is crucial for clarity. Be sure to name who is doing what, and when it will be done.

In the case of student discipline, this would include any follow-up teaching that is going to occur, adjustments to the behavior plan, assigned consequences, restorative conversations, etc. When talking to Strike's parents, it might sound like this:

"Strike will be out of school the next two days. When he returns, he has agreed to a facilitated restorative conversation with the other student and the coach. Our counselor, Mr. Harken, will meet with all parties in advance to prepare them for the conversation and then he will facilitate it.

Strike is to have no contact with the other student until the restorative conversation. There are likely going to be additional actions that Strike will need to take in order to make repairs. This will be determined in the restorative conversations. Mr. Harken will also see if he can help Strike identify what is at the root of his behavior change these last few months.

Thank you for agreeing to have a conversation with Strike about the recent changes. If these attempts by you and Mr. Harken are unsuccessful, you have agreed to pursue outside counseling. I will send you the notes from this meeting, including these action steps by the end of the day for your records."

Then, don't forget to send that email. When addressing educator performance we would discuss both the action plan for the teacher and the planned support from the administrator. It might sound like this:

"Thank you for working with me on this today. I appreciate that you agreed to visit Ms. Jones on Tuesday with our instructional coach and observe how she is implementing the phonics curriculum. The instructional coach will observe you implementing the curriculum by the end of the week. I look forward to coming and observing implementation on Tuesday of the following week.

When we are done here, I will connect you and the instructional coach so she knows what we are asking her to do. I will also send you a summary of this conversation so we can make sure we don't lose track of any of these details."

What if there is disagreement about an action that you are going to require? That is when we explicitly state the expectation. We may use the broken record technique, saying the same thing each time they refuse or state a reason not to it. These words and phrases can be extremely helpful when reinforcing an expectation that the educator or caregiver is reluctant to embrace:

- Nevertheless
- Even so
- All the same
- Regardless
- And yet

For example, "I understand that you do not like the new phonics curriculum. And yet, all second-grade teachers are required to implement this evidence-based tool." The teacher may respond with why she should stick with her previous curriculum again. At that point we restate exactly what was said above. Rinse and repeat as needed. In thinking about the conversation regarding Strike, it might sound like, "I hear that you are frustrated that Strike will be suspended for two days. Nevertheless, when a student hits another student, they must be removed from school for a period of time in accordance with district policy."

Follow-Up in Writing

We know that two people can leave a conversation with two different ideas about what is going to happen next. This is why we recommend following up in writing. This provides an opportunity for clarity, and creates a written record. In this email, include the main points that were discussed in the meeting, the action plan that has been established, and the expectations moving forward. By being thorough in this message, you aren't leaving room for misunderstanding. You also now have written documentation if the expectations are not met or should the behavior repeat.

Pulling It All Together

Let's take a look at the example of Ms. Embed, who is struggling with utilizing the new phonics curriculum. The administrator may say something like:

> "It is time to start wrapping this up. I am thankful that we agree that the results of the most recent reading benchmark assessment indicate that your students are not making expected growth. We also agree that school board policy requires that teachers use the board-adopted curriculum. I know that you prefer the curriculum from last year, because it is easier for you to use and you felt students found it more engaging. Nevertheless, the expectation is that you use the curriculum that has been adopted by the school board as recommended by the Literacy Adoption Committee.
>
> Thank you for working with me on this today. I appreciate that you are going to visit Ms. Jones this Tuesday with our instructional coach, Mr. Bolster. Together, you will discuss how she is implementing the phonics curriculum. Mr. Bolster will offer feedback on your implementation by the end of the week. I look forward to observing you next week on Thursday during the literacy block.
>
> When we are done here, I will send an email to you and Mr. Bolster so he knows his part in this plan. I will also

send you a separate summary of this conversation so we can make sure we don't lose track of any of these details. I appreciate you meeting with me, I will see you this afternoon at the staff meeting."

The email that you send is going to sound remarkably similar. We will include more detail that includes all the important facts. For the teacher above, it would look like this:

Dear Ms. Embed,

Thank you for meeting with me this morning to discuss the use of the adopted reading curriculum. We reviewed your students' progress on the most recent benchmark assessment and agreed that it was less than expected progress.

As we discussed in the meeting, I have observed you on three occasions using the outdated reading curriculum from last year during the reading block. During this time, we are expected to use the new board-adopted curriculum, including the direct phonics instruction that is embedded. In all three cases, I shared the importance of you using the new curriculum. When we met today, you shared that you have not been using the new curriculum because you find it to be more challenging to navigate, and you feel your students are more engaged when using the other curriculum. Regardless, you acknowledge that it is school board policy to use the adopted curriculum and this is the expectation going forward.

In order to support you with this we built an action plan:

- I will arrange for you to have a half-day sub on Tuesday. During that time you are going to visit Ms. Jones with Mr. Bolster and observe how she is implementing the phonics curriculum.
- You will meet with Mr. Bolster after that observation and go through all of the tools in the new curriculum so he can answer any questions about how to use it.
- Mr. Bolster will observe you implementing the curriculum by the end of the week and will provide you with feedback and coaching.
- I will be coming to observe during the literacy block on Thursday of the following week.
- You will use the adopted curriculum daily during the literacy block, including the phonics instruction.

Thank you for taking this seriously. I am happy to provide any additional clarification that is needed.

Respectfully,

Dr. K

When You Have to End the Meeting

When it is clear to you that the meeting needs to end and the other person is in no rush to do so, there are a few things you can do. First, go through the summary above to bring closure to the meeting. If at that point they are stuck, or want to rehash further, stick to the broken record technique and repeat the expectation. We also recommend the following sentence stems:

- We need to start wrapping up now.
- At this point, we need to conclude.
- It is time to wrap this up.

After you have made it clear the meeting is over, head toward the door. Open it, and invite them to leave ahead of you.

Connecting It

How we end the meeting will have a significant impact on the success of our Connected Conversation. Point out the areas of agreement as a building block for the next steps. Be clear on what everyone is expected to do as a result of the meeting, and then follow up in writing as needed. No one deserves that, and it is unproductive to allow it to continue. Wrapping it up is an important skill. Use it to ensure clarity of expectations and next steps.

Connected Takeaways

- Include identified points of agreement as you wrap up.
- Be explicit about next steps for everyone in the conversation.
- Be clear about any expectations moving forward.
- Follow up in writing.

Coaching for the Big Moments

CHAPTER 13

Up or Out: Coaching with Purpose

*"Do the best you can until you know better.
Then when you know better, do better."*

–Maya Angelou

Have you ever heard the phrase, "hire well, fire well"? Well, Erika and Tiffany have. We originally heard this in our administrative program and it left us with a lot of questions. After much discussion, we determined it is missing a critical component: coaching. Unfortunately, we have witnessed many leaders skip coaching and move immediately to dismissal when they notice a staff member who is in need of significant improvement. We believe strong leaders *start* with coaching. There are times to coach for improvement, and

> Strong leaders *start* with coaching.

there are times to coach someone to a new path, or as we like to say, "Coach 'em up or coach 'em out."

Small disclaimer before we go any further. There are times that coaching is not appropriate, and we simply need to move to dismissal. This includes gross misconduct, unethical behavior, or putting student safety at risk. When this is the case, call Human Resources and go through the process. Thankfully, these cases are rare. In this chapter, we will focus on the more common times when coaching is your best bet.

Coaching Up

When, over time, we see that an educator is not meeting expectations—with classroom management, student achievement, attitude, paperwork, building relationships, etc., we bring this to their attention as soon as we observe it. Then, we coach up. This might include observing classrooms together, offering resources, providing a mentor, additional time, or curricular tools. Most often when we are clear in our expectations, provide supports, and give consistent feedback, the coaching works. When the educator is reflective, open to coaching, incorporates changes into their practice, and begins to make visible improvements, it is incredibly rewarding.

Recently, a principal colleague was supporting a second-year teacher. There were some significant gaps in pedagogy and lesson planning that had been noted and discussed the previous year. As part of the coaching plan, the principal scheduled regular time with the educator, discussed pedagogy, co-planned a unit, reviewed lesson plans weekly, and gave clear and consistent feedback on their progress. By the end of the year, the teacher had made so much growth that they moved from Needs Improvement to Highly Effective in these areas of the rubric. The principal was then thrilled to renew their contract with confidence and enthusiasm.

Coaching Them Up or Out?

How do you know it's time to consider coaching someone out? This is such a challenging and stressful thing for leaders to navigate. We invest so much time and energy into the staff we supervise. We have spoken to countless educators who find this process to be wrought with self-doubt, worry, and second guessing. These are the decisions that keep us up at night.

There are a variety of reasons that we might coach out instead of up. Regardless of the reason, it is important that you have done all you can to coach them up. If that hasn't worked, it's either a lack of will or a lack of skill. With a lack of will, the educator refuses coaching. They simply do not have the will to improve, or do not accept that the changes are necessary. In the case of skill, the educator is open to changing, but despite our coaching and their effort, their skill set is simply not a match for their role. It could be that the subject area, specialty, or age group is not a fit for them. Perhaps education is simply not the career for them.

When you are starting to believe it is time to coach out, we encourage you to challenge your thinking by checking with another confidential administrator or mentor. Talk through your thought process, or even consider asking them to observe the teacher. They may be able to identify a strategy or support you may have missed.

After providing extensive coaching, support, and checking your thinking with a trusted colleague, it will be easier to sleep at night knowing you have done all you can. This does not mean moving to coaching out will be easy to do, but it does make the decision more clear. After all, as Mae West said, "I never said it would be easy, I only said it would be worth it."

Connecting It

Strong leaders prioritize coaching. Staff members deserve the gift of feedback and support. When that does not move practice forward, either due to a lack of will or skill, we must transition to coaching them out. When you believe it is time to transition to coaching-out, check your thinking with a trusted colleague, and then get ready for the hard work described in the following chapters.

Connected Takeaways

- Strong leaders believe in coaching up and doing all they can before moving to coaching out.
- Check your thinking on coaching up or out with a trusted colleague.
- We coach out after we have exhausted our resources and see that there is a lack of will or skill to improve.

CHAPTER 14

Putting Coaching Out into Action

"We must be headlights and not tail lights."

–John Lewis

Simply put, coaching someone out is not fun. It can be quite the stressful and anxiety-provoking process. And yet, it's a necessary one. Once we determine we are going to proceed with coaching someone out, we must continually check in with ourselves to ensure that we are staying true to our values. No matter what, remember to treat the person with dignity, communicate directly, and have compassion throughout the process.

Be Direct with the Facts

When coaching someone out, it is necessary to share information directly. It does not help anyone to sugar coat the message. We must continually remind them of the expectations and then communicate clearly that they are not meeting them. Rely on your evaluation tool and use it as a third point. Make sure to provide concrete examples in written and verbal communication. Remember—we don't do gotchas and we don't do surprises. Remind them of the timelines you have established for improvement. One of the many conversations while coaching someone out might sound like:

"Mr. Kaos, as we have discussed on several occasions, I am concerned about classroom management as shown here on strand 2b and 2c of the teacher evaluation rubric. You agreed that your current practice does not meet expectations according to the rubric.

You indicated that you found it helpful to observe Ms. Groove's classroom on three occasions and you stated that you observed effective modeling of transitions and classroom management strategies. You also have had ongoing meetings with your mentor teacher, Mr. Bolster, who has supported you with how to establish routines and strategies to create a more safe and calm learning environment.

Yesterday when I observed, I did not see the improvement that we were expecting. It did not appear as though the strategies from Ms. Groove or Mr. Bolster were being used. The transitions are taking between five and seven minutes, the students talked over you when you were giving directions, two students shoved each other in the corner, a pencil was thrown, and one student slept the entire time I was in the room. Not only was the environment unsafe, there was also very little learning occurring.

You have been given much support that we collaboratively identified, yet it's not showing up in your practice. I want you to be successful and provide the support you need, but so far it's not working. I'm worried."

Probing Questions

Ask probing questions and provide plenty of space to help them self-identify where they are. Truth be told, these questions aren't always the easiest to ask. However, they have been pivotal in our success in coaching people out in a compassionate way. Probing questions provide an opportunity for the educator to genuinely reflect on their practice and satisfaction with their work. We can't tell you the number of times these conversations have helped a staff member realize their current role wasn't a good fit and they needed to make a change.

Here are some examples that have worked for us:

- How are you going to make significant improvements?
- How do you feel about your performance?
- Are you happy in this position?
- Do you feel effective?
- Are you feeling like this job is a good match for your skill set?
- What do you see as a path forward?

When asking these questions provide plenty of wait time. Don't jump in to save them. This can be challenging, especially as empathetic humans. When we notice someone sitting in discomfort, it can be tempting to jump in and try and help them feel better. We aren't suggesting you be rude or unkind, but don't soften the message. Give them the opportunity to truly reflect on their performance. State what you noticed, how it is falling short of expectations, pose your questions, and then *be quiet and listen.*

> **Provide plenty of wait time. Don't jump in to save them.**

If the teacher responds by agreeing with your assessment, whatever you do, don't minimize the problem or tell them that everything is fine. Agree with them, nod your head, thank them for their vulnerability and candor. Allow them to talk, reflect, and process out loud. If needed, ask more probing questions that cause genuine introspection. If they share that they are worried or scared or feel incompetent, acknowledge and validate that. Sit with them quietly. Don't try to change their mind.

Lack of Skill

Consider Mr. Kaos from the previous example, and imagine he shares the following:

> "Yeah. I noticed that, too. It was a little out of control and I just don't know how to fix it. I did watch Ms. Groove, but she's been teaching so long, I just don't feel comfy telling middle schoolers to sit down and be quiet. Mr.

Bolster has talked to me a lot about my tone and volume, but I just can't figure out how to talk more firmly. It's just not in my nature. There's just so much to pay attention to and I truly don't know how to do it. I feel awful and I'm so frustrated. I feel like maybe I'm just never going to be able to do this."

Here is your opening. Pause and let the weight of their own words hang in the air. Nod empathetically. After a few beats, respond by saying:

"I'm so sorry you are feeling frustrated and awful and like you aren't going to be able to do this. That must be worrisome and stressful. You've been working hard for months now and you aren't making the improvements we need to see. I know you want to be effective and you're upset that you aren't getting the results that we were hoping for. I can see how unhappy you are. I'm not quite sure how we can move forward here. What do you think?"

Instead of softening the message, you are acknowledging and validating their feelings, while still being clear. It is often in these moments that staff members decide to resign. The key is to continue to state the expectation, provide clear and direct feedback on the progress (or lack thereof), pose probing questions, and then give them space in the conversation to sit with the hard truth. By allowing them space to come to this realization, we are treating them with dignity. Remember, in this situation, students are not learning, nor is their environment safe. Mr. Kaos thinks he's ineffective in his role. Honestly? He's not wrong. Everyone will be happier if he chooses a path that is a better match for his skill set.

Give them space in the conversation to sit with the hard truth.

Lack of Will

Now let's take a look at an example where the lack of progress is more a lack of will than skill. Let's say you are coaching a middle school social studies teacher who relies solely on lecture as a means of sharing information. Let's call her Ms. Verbose. Students are not performing well on external assessments. Both students and caregivers have begun complaining about her. When sharing your observation feedback with Ms. Verbose, the conversation might sound like this:

> "As I have shared on several occasions, I'm concerned about student engagement, shown on strand 3a and 3b of the evaluation rubric. When I observed the lesson yesterday, I noticed that you spoke about the topic for twenty-five minutes.

> During that time, four students were staring out the window, and did not take any notes. One student was drawing with a sharpie on his hand and had his earbuds in. One student was asleep with her head on her desk. Two students were passing notes to one another in the back corner of the room. One student asked to use the restroom and did not return the entire time I was there (I did text the dean to check in on him after fifteen minutes had passed).

At no point did I observe you pausing the lecture to check for understanding. Additionally, you did not stop to ask the students to reflect on any of the material, nor did you ask them what questions they had.

I'm concerned because the students were not given an opportunity to engage with the content. We need our students to make meaning of the material and I'm just not seeing that happening. Did I miss how you were assessing whether students understood the content?"

Let's imagine the teacher replies:

"No, you didn't. That wasn't part of today's plan. This lesson was a lecture on the chapter they were supposed to have read last night. I assigned an essay to write for homework tonight and that will let me know if they understood the material or not. My guess is they didn't and it's very likely that many of them will not even complete the essay.

You know, I'm concerned, too. Well over half the students are failing my class and it's just a tragedy. It appears that this generation of students simply does not have the capacity to listen, pay attention, or even give the slightest bit of effort when it doesn't suit them. My job is not to entertain them. My job is to teach the material. It's just not my fault that they can't absorb information from a lecture. They are refusing to take responsibility for any of their own learning. I mean, honestly, they are all so interested in their cell phones and video games, and, as you said, note passing. How can I compete with that?

Also, the students you mentioned who were staring out the window? You know what they were looking at? They were watching the alt ed kids plant in the garden near the window. It's such a distraction. How can I be expected to teach when they are out there playing with shovels and throwing dirt? You know, I brought this up at the meeting earlier this fall. I said that ridiculous garden would be a huge distraction and guess what? It looks like it is. What is administration going to do about that garden outside my classroom?"

Breathe deep and for goodness sake, don't take the bait and follow the teacher down this rabbit hole. This tactic is a red herring, and it is very important not to get defensive or sidetracked. Stay focused on the issue at hand. State the expectation again and ensure the responsibility remains with them. Respond like this:

"I hear your frustration. If you'd like to have another meeting about the garden, please reach out to our office manager to set up a meeting with me. At the moment, we are discussing the lack of engagement with the students in your class.

Our job is to teach the students in front of us. If students don't have an opportunity to engage with the material, they won't learn it. I'm sure it's not your intention, but it sounds like you are blaming the students for not learning the material.

I wholeheartedly believe that we need to have high standards and high expectations for our students. I also agree with you that students need to take ownership of their learning and they need to be held accountable when they are making poor choices.

However, today I didn't see any misbehavior from the students. What I saw was nearly a third of your class disengaged. We've discussed this several times and I'm really worried.

One of the roles of a teacher is to ensure that students are engaged with the material being taught. As you can see on 3a and 3b on the rubric, this is not happening. The teaching methods you are using are not effective for the class. This aligns to the Does Not Meet area of the rubric. We appear to be at an impasse. What do you see as a path forward?"

At this point, the teacher may argue and restate their view or try to direct the conversation elsewhere. This is a time that we suggest relying on the broken record technique. Repeat the expectation, reference the rubric as a third point, and restate your concern.

If the teacher is unwilling to admit they need to change, you don't have to continue to look for possible supports or solutions. At this point, that is their responsibility, not yours. If the teacher will not agree to make changes or even agree that changes need to be made, then you'll need to direct them to do so. Stay strong here and remember that your most important role is to support student learning. You might say:

"I'm sorry we are unable to agree that a change needs to be made in regard to your teaching practice. At this point, I am directing you to incorporate more engaging strategies, such as think-pair-share, asking probing and clarifying questions, and providing opportunities for students to talk and engage with the material and each other so they can make meaning of the material being presented. I'll be back in on Thursday and I will be looking for engagement strategies."

If on Thursday you still don't see a change, then you'll need to begin the process of putting the teacher on a formal plan of improvement.

Documentation

We cannot overstate the importance of documentation during this process. Regardless if we are coaching up or coaching out, documentation is not only our friend—it's our lifeline. When someone is under stress and hearing about areas to improve, we should assume that they will not remember everything we discussed. We recommend ending every conversation with a recap of the next steps along with the dates and other specific information. Then, let them know that you will follow up with an email summarizing the conversation so they can have this in writing.

> **CTC Tip:** When sending a summary of conversation email, bcc yourself and save that in a folder in your email. This allows you to quickly refer back to the information when you need it, instead of having to hunt through your sent email to find the documentation.

When You Have to Fire Someone

Sometimes we do everything we can to coach them out and it just doesn't work. In these cases, we'll need to move to termination. Before doing so, we want to ask ourselves if we have done everything we could to support this staff member. Were we clear with expectations? Did we give specific feedback? Did we provide ongoing and consistent support? Did we seek other opinions? If we answered yes to all these questions and they simply did not respond to our coaching, it's time to move to termination. It is crucial that you work closely with HR and follow the official termination process. Thankfully, you'll be able to rely on the extensive documentation you have collected to make the process a bit smoother.

An example of this that hits home for Erika involves a chance encounter. Early in her career, Erika was struggling to support a long-time employee whose performance was significantly suffering as a result of a number of difficult circumstances. Erika cared deeply about this person, while also being very troubled by the impact this change was having on students. She spent hours planning for, practicing, and engaging in the conversations that were needed during this difficult period. In the end, before Erika moved to termination, the employee decided to resign. Unfortunately, they were also pretty angry.

Many years later, Erika ran into this person in the community. She approached Erika, gave her a huge hug, and thanked her for pushing her into the change that was needed, opening her up to do work that was a better fit. She also shared that although she was extremely angry at the time, looking back she can clearly see that she had been treated fairly and with dignity throughout. This moment reminded

Erika why the time, energy, effort, and even occasional lost sleep is so worth it.

Connecting It

Coaching someone out isn't fun, but it is necessary. We must be clear in our expectations and share concrete evidence. Ask probing questions to help them see the areas for improvement. Once you determine if it's a lack of will or skill, use that information to coach them out. Make sure to keep documenting everything along the way and send a summary of conversation after every meeting. The documentation will be helpful if, in the end, you need to move to termination.

Connected Takeaways

- Coaching out is a necessary part of leadership.
- Be crystal clear with facts and don't hold back information.
- Ask probing questions to encourage reflection.
- Determine if the problem is a lack of will or skill.
- Document, document, document.
- If it becomes time to move to termination, work closely with HR and follow the process carefully.

CHAPTER 15

Protecting the Culture: Coaching Negative Staff

"Negativity is contagious. Unhappiness is contagious. Fear is contagious. But so is optimism. So is happiness. So is love. Surround yourself with people who bring out the best in you. And strive to be a reflection of what you want to receive."

–Michell C. Clark

Have you ever worked with a negative, toxic staff member who causes you to reconsider your chosen profession? We are talking about staff who can't find anything positive to say and are often quick to turn negative, especially in public spaces. These are staff who consistently look for problems over solutions or frequently speak poorly of students, families, staff, or the school. To be clear, we aren't saying that staff should never share something negative. Nor are we encouraging toxic positivity. We have chosen a challenging profession. Of course we are going to have bad days, and sometimes we need to vent. That's not what we are talking about here. We are talking about staff members who feel that most days are bad days and venting is a near daily occurrence. If you have the misfortune to work with these staff, you know exactly to whom we are referring.

You are Who You Eat Lunch With

You know when you arrive at work, randomly wearing the same color or style of clothing as your work bestie? Or when you find yourself finishing your colleagues' sentences? This is due to a fascinating process called neural synchronization. Neural synchronization is when our brain syncs up with the people around us. The more time we spend with someone, the more this synchronization happens. After a while, the pathways in our brain actually change, causing us to be more similar to people we spend the most time with. It's why we like to say, "You are who you eat lunch with."

Think about the various individuals you see throughout the school day. How do they make you feel? For us, there are some educators who consistently energize, excite, and inspire us. There are others who seem to spread a sense of negativity and frustration everywhere they go. Unfortunately, these negative folks tend to have a stronger influence on our emotions. Why is that?

Well, it turns out, we all have a negativity bias, making negative emotions easier to catch than positive ones. In *Culturally Responsive Teaching and the Brain (2015)*, Zaretta Hammond shares, ". . . the brain is more than 20 times more focused on negative experiences than on positive ones." (p. 66) As the school leader, we need to be very aware of the influence different educators have on the culture. Be careful to separate pockets of negativity, and ensure that newer or more impressionable staff are surrounded by positive influences.

Understanding the disproportionate impacts of negativity means that it is especially important for us to address it and fast.

> Be careful to separate pockets of negativity

Consider the True Impact

One of the most unfair parts of working with some toxic teachers is that sometimes, although they have a negative impact on the school culture, they may be strong in the classroom. In these cases, they likely have been in education for a long time and may even have quite the long line of fans.

If we think about coaching out, we may start to feel guilty and think, "But they are not *that* bad. They get good achievement results. It's selfish for me to take them out of the classroom; they only impact me." So you plod along, try to ignore the impact on climate, work to anticipate their complaints, and spend hours and hours of time contemplating how to work *around* them in order to move initiatives forward, support other staff, or just get your job done. Meanwhile, you are sending a strong and clear message to the rest of your staff: This person is actually leading our school.

We want to encourage you to consider the time you spend trying to placate this person. When introducing something new that you or the district wants to implement, do you immediately wonder how badly this staff member will respond? How much energy do you spend just thinking about how to work around this one person? We are going to guess a lot of time. Perhaps even more time than you are willing to admit to yourself. Now, if you were able to recapture that time, energy, and focus, imagine how many staff members you could coach up.

We must also consider how many great teachers leave due to this toxicity. How many potential amazing leaders decided *not* to go into leadership positions because they watched this toxic struggle and did not want to take it on? Is missing out on other great educators good for kids? No, it isn't. If you are forced to make this decision, we hope you now have the permission you need to coach them out. They are a bully. No matter how great a teacher they are. Or how close to retirement they may be.

CTC Tip: Consider someone's propensity for positivity when hiring. Tiffany's school hired staff using three tenets: 1. They love kids. 2. They love working on a team. 3. They are experts in their field. Guess how many of those you can coach for? You guessed it. Just one. You can absolutely support someone to become an excellent teacher. You can work with them to grow and improve their practice with PD, book studies, and mentors. You cannot teach someone to love kids and you cannot convince someone to see the value of working on a team.

Call It When You See It

So, what do you do if you have a teacher who is consistently problem-focused, negative, and has a toxic impact on the culture? You can't really offer professional development on how to not be so grumpy. It's also not likely that a mentor can coach them out of it. It is likely, however, that the mentor could be sucked into their negativity.

So, instead, call it when you see it and actually name it. Lean on your rubric. Focus on the areas that address collaboration or professionalism. Find specific examples of when they are displaying this behavior and document it–continuously. Set regular meetings for check-ins and keep holding them to the expectation. Ideally, they will be reflective and make changes. But what to do if that doesn't happen?

Peer Pressure

Share with the teacher their negative impact on other staff. This is crucial. Not only do you want to isolate the staff member to protect others from the toxicity, you also want the staff member to hear how their words and actions influence others. This shouldn't be a secret. If staff are feeling uncomfortable and it's impacting the culture, you'll need to address it directly. Sometimes hearing that their colleagues are bringing it forward as a concern is just the peer pressure they need to change their behavior. We have seen this work many times.

Isolate

It's very important that positive staff members don't decide to isolate themselves. In fact, you'll actually want the opposite to occur. You want the positive members of staff congregating and connecting. You want the negative staff members to isolate. So, help them. Is there a negative group in one area of the building? Do a few staff members who regularly complain together have the same prep or supervision duty? Split them up. Change their prep, switch their duties, and consider reassigning their rooms. You might ask, "Well, won't they know what I'm doing?" Our response: Yes! This is an appropriate time to name your motivation directly. Again, this should not be a secret, and it is good for them to see that you are holding them accountable. This doesn't need to be sneaky. In fact, it *shouldn't* be sneaky. This might sound like:

> "One of our stated values is that we will communicate in a positive and collaborative way with one another at school. I have been made aware that you are interacting negatively and in a way that is not collaborative or solution-focused. I am deeply concerned about how this is impacting our culture. Instead of contributing positively, ensuring this is a place where people want to come to work and students want to come to school, the environment feels less collegial.
>
> Three staff members this week shared with me that your continued comments in the staff room about how students are spoiled and entitled made them feel uncomfortable. One staff member shared that she is not comfortable talking about the positive things kids do because of how you might respond.
>
> I have an obligation to cultivate a caring and professional work environment so I need to take steps to disrupt this behavior. Moving forward, I want you to consider how you speak about students and refrain from discussing them in a negative manner.

Additionally, I am going to switch your supervision duty to the morning and move your prep to the afternoon to reduce the impact your attitude is having on others. What other steps might you take to improve this negative culture that you are contributing to?"

That sounds like a big conversation, doesn't it? Well, you're right. It is. We don't have a lot of modeling for this because people don't typically talk this directly about negative or toxic behavior. We encourage you to ask yourself why that might be. When coaching negative staff, we ensure clarity, hold firm on our expectations, and consistently offer feedback.

We don't have to tiptoe around the behavior just because it's more challenging to pinpoint. We remind ourselves how much damage they are causing. We don't have to be overly concerned about the discomfort they may feel when we call them on it. After all, discomfort is often a great motivator for change.

> We don't have to tiptoe around the behavior just because it's more challenging to pinpoint.

We were once talking to a principal who shared a story from early in his career. He was trying everything he could think of to coach up a negative staff member, who we will call Mr. Gloomy. He offered praise, public shout outs, support with schedule, curriculum, planning, etc. Nothing worked. At the end-of-the-year celebration, the principal chose one staff member to highlight for everyone. Who did he pick? You guessed it, Mr. Gloomy. People were stunned. Positive staff lost trust. Negative staff were emboldened, and Mr. Gloomy was recognized for displaying unprofessional behavior. And did it encourage Mr. Gloomy to stop complaining and gossiping about other staff and students? It most certainly did not. The principal lamented to us that recognizing Mr. Gloomy was a mistake, and after some careful reflection with his mentor, he took another approach and began to isolate Mr. Gloomy. He no longer received public appreciation or praise. He was not selected to represent the staff at district meetings. He stopped being looked at as a leader on staff. The principal clearly articulated his concerns, documented appropriately, provided consistent feedback, and ended up coaching out Mr. Gloomy. Was it fun? No. Was it necessary? Absolutely. And did the whole staff let out a giant sigh of relief at the first staff meeting without Mr. Gloomy? You betcha.

Connecting It

Emotions are contagious and negative emotions are especially so. When faced with a staff member who is especially negative, we must consider the true impact they are having on their colleagues and our school culture. We also have to call it when we see it and clearly name the negative behavior. Use peer pressure to help staff understand how their behavior is affecting colleagues and culture. If despite all of your efforts that doesn't work, do what you can to isolate the staff member to lessen their impact on others and begin to take steps to coach them out.

Connected Takeaways

- It's easier to catch negative emotions than positive ones.
- Negative staff members can quickly create a toxic school culture.
- When you notice a staff member being consistently negative, clearly name it along with your expectations that it changes.
- Share how the negative behavior is impacting other staff or the culture.
- Take steps to isolate the staff member and lessen their impact.

CHAPTER 16

Coaching with Leverage: The Evaluation Process

"For teachers, as for students, the most effective evaluation comes from someone who sits besides us and helps us grow"

–Carol Ann Tomlinson

Be honest. When you think about the evaluation process, do you think about it as an opportunity to propel growth, or do you see it as a pesky task on your to-do list? For many of us, the evaluation process has become another irritating and time-consuming duty that lacks meaning or only feels necessary for someone who is truly struggling. If this resonates, we're excited to shift your thinking. In reality, this can be one of the most high-leverage processes we have to impact educator effectiveness. As an added bonus, celebrating teacher effectiveness and student growth is incredibly meaningful and rewarding. However, as with most all we do, the way in which we communicate throughout this process is paramount.

Start with Goals

As educators, our main charge is to improve student achievement and ensure that our students have the necessary knowledge and skills to be successful. This means that everything we do should be in service to this. One way to do this is through a goal-setting process.

It is powerful when all our goals are in alignment. Individual student goals should align to teacher goals and those should align to school and district goals. Throughout the process, we need to ensure that we are aiming high. Low goals get low results. If you are hoping to raise student achievement, start by raising the bar. It's not as simple as high goals equating to high achievement, but you can be certain that low goals will result in low achievement.

Part of the goal setting process is discussing with each individual teacher what support is needed for the teacher to reach their ambitious goals. As leaders, it is our job to provide the resources and tools to get there. Teachers can't reach their goals if we aren't providing the needed support throughout the process.

Goal setting should be a collaborative process. During goal-setting conferences, lean on the questions below to encourage deeper reflection and support to identify highly rigorous goals.

If the goal is too vague:

- How will you know if you've met this goal by the end of the year?
- What specific student outcomes will show progress?
- Can we make this measurable so we can track growth?

If the goal lacks rigor:

- Does this target push student learning far enough?
- What would this goal look like if we raised expectations to match grade-level standards?
- If all students met this goal, would it significantly move our School Improvement Plan (SIP) targets?

If the goal doesn't align to schoolwide priorities:

- How does this goal connect to our PLC or SIP priorities?
- What adjustments could we make so your goal reinforces the team's focus?
- How might aligning this goal with our schoolwide fluency focus give your students extra support?

If the teacher needs support in instruction, management, or culture:

- What strategies would help bring more clarity to your instruction?
- How can your goal support consistent classroom management routines?
- What steps could you take to strengthen classroom positivity and relationships?

> **CTC Tip:** If you meet as an administrative team, it can be super helpful to review teacher goals prior to the conference. You might even consider collecting teacher goals and analyzing them as a team. This helps to ensure that you are calibrated and have similar expectations of staff. It can also provide you with an opportunity to role play these conversations prior to holding them.

The Final Evaluation

The purpose of the end-of-year conference is to reflect and review. You'll want to begin the conference by discussing their progress toward meeting the goals that were set at the beginning of the year. The conversation should be focused on the specific strategies that supported them in meeting their goals or reasons why they did not. Either way, this analysis will help us determine next steps for the following year.

It's important to remember the final evaluation conference is not the place to raise new concerns, or rehash resolved issues. You need to ensure that you have provided frequent and ongoing feedback. If you have not, it's not fair to wait until the end-of-year conference to evaluate them based on a new concern they have not yet had an opportunity to address. You can, however, bring up the concern and let them know that you look forward to supporting them with it in the following year.

Choosing the Area of Focus

In order to best leverage the final evaluation conference, we want to carefully consider the most impactful area for improvement. Take some time to review the evaluation rubric, classroom observations, data team notes, student achievement data, or any other objective information that can help you determine a focus area. Notice we are recommending one area of focus. You may be thinking, "Well, this teacher needs to focus on a number of areas." If that is the case, hold tight, we address this later in the chapter.

Consider Ms. Green, a newer teacher who is finding her way. As we are preparing for her final evaluation conference, we reflect back on her instructional practice and professional demeanor during the year and several areas of concern come to mind. She had quite a struggle with the math curriculum and her students' test scores in math were well below what is expected. In November she had a challenging encounter with a parent that she did not handle well. Thankfully, after you spoke to her, her caregiver communication improved, and there were no further issues. Finally, this spring, she frequently set up dynamic and engaging, hands-on science labs that required a lot of clean-up from the nighttime custodian. The custodian had asked you to talk to her about this a few times and you simply haven't had the conversation with her yet. Should we address all three concerns during her final evaluation conference? Our recommendation is no. If we were to discuss all three, we may overwhelm the teacher and she may not know where to begin.

Don't Muddy Your Message

One year, Tiffany had a new supervisor. During her end-of-year evaluation conference, the supervisor gave in-depth and extensive feedback. He gave her marks of "Meets" or "Exceeds" standards across the board. However, he also gave her two to three items to improve on in *each* area of the rubric. All told, there were twenty-five suggestions for improvement! Not only was this overwhelming, but it was also defeating. Tiffany wasn't quite sure what to prioritize. She was also confused. Her evaluation ratings were high and yet, there were so many areas to focus on. That summer she identified specific strategies to respond to each point. She listed these out and presented them to her supervisor the following fall. The supervisor was baffled. He literally asked, "Why on earth did you create this? You are doing so well. What made you think you needed to give me this list?" Tiffany explained that the feedback given during her evaluation conference made her think she had much to improve despite having such high ratings. The supervisor shared that his comments were merely suggestions—not directives. Turns out, suggestions during an evaluation process are received as directives. There isn't a way for them to be heard differently.

> Suggestions during an evaluation process are received as directives.

The words of a supervisor during an evaluation conference carry significantly more weight than in a regular coaching conversation. Use this to your advantage. Don't muddy your message by sharing every possible way to improve. Choose your words intentionally, and be strategic. Select the highest leverage area to focus on and make that crystal clear.

High Leverage Areas of Focus

So—thinking back to Ms. Green. For this conversation, we suggest the principal consider what patterns or generalizations exist. Did Ms. Green fail to respond in a timely manner to many parents or was it just this one time? Happily, she responded to the coaching and it didn't happen again. That being the case, what's the point of bringing it up now? If it had been a pattern, then it would make sense to document it in her evaluation. Since it didn't, we'll move on.

Unfortunately, the labs that require clean-up from the custodian are a pattern. However, at this point, Ms. Green doesn't yet know they are causing any issues for anyone. It's a relatively easy fix for Ms. Green to do a better job tidying-up so all the cleaning isn't left for the already over-worked custodian. Should this be addressed with Ms. Green? Yes, for sure. But during her evaluation conference? No, this isn't the time. This would be better as drop-in conversation at another time.

It is clear that Ms. Green's struggles with the math curriculum and the resulting lackluster scores is the most important point to address during the conference. Now that we know *what* we are planning to talk about, let's dive in.

Having the Conversation

Show up at the meeting prepared with all the needed information, data, timeline of previous conversations, and support provided. Be clear about the expected progress and where they are currently performing. Guide the conversation toward the determined area of focus.

With Ms. Green, we'll show the math data. This is a time where the third point can be extremely helpful. Discuss the support provided and make sure to include times that you have previously brought these concerns to her attention. You'll also want to point out how that correlates with the teacher evaluation rubric. The actual conversation might sound like this:

"In these areas, you did not meet expectations. As you remember, in the fall during our Data Day meetings, we discussed the low scores for the math benchmark assessments. At that time, we discussed having an additional educational assistant placed in your classroom to support more tiered groups for instruction.

We also identified the students to receive Tier II math instruction with the Math Intervention Teacher during your intervention & extension block. When your students still weren't making expected progress on our common assessment later in October, we met and I shared concerns with you then. You stated that you were struggling with the math curriculum. We then scheduled a time for you to meet weekly with the math instructional coach. You also attended a math conference in early winter to help you with additional instructional strategies.

In January, after the winter benchmarking assessment results were available, I shared my deep concerns due to the fact that the number of students who were meeting benchmark had actually decreased and the number of students at-risk had significantly increased. We provided a half-day sub so you and I could meet with the Math

Intervention Teacher and the Math Coach to brainstorm groupings, instructional strategies, and other supports. In looking at the end-of-year summative assessment, it shows that sixty-seven percent of the students in your class did not meet standard.

I'm worried, Ms. Green. As we've discussed several times, it is imperative that our students make strong growth and learn the needed skills in second grade in order to be successful for next year and beyond. At this point, well over half of the students are one to two years below grade level and will be starting third grade at a significant disadvantage. I'm thinking about next year, and I'm really concerned. We will need to see a significant change in the math instruction and scores early next year because right now the learning of our students is suffering. In the fall when we meet again, you will be placed on a plan of assistance to improve math instruction."

Now, let's imagine a teacher who is showing results like these and also has a number of issues in other areas of their instruction or professionalism. If there are many areas needing improvement, the teacher is not appearing to be coachable, and we've discussed these concerns previously, then we do something completely different. This is when we might consider using the kitchen sink approach.

In this case, we include all the areas that need improvement and we discuss them again during the conference. We then review each area, one by one, and describe how they will be included in the formalized plan of improvement the following year. Might this be overwhelming? Yes, it might. Might it cause them to reconsider their grade level, content area, specialty, or even chosen profession? Possibly. And yet, one of the most compassionate things we can do as leaders is to help people recognize when they are in the wrong spot.

Supporting Highly Effective Educators

Our highly effective staff members need coaching too. Although it can be tempting to just offer praise, don't rob them of the opportunity to continue to grow. They don't necessarily need us to offer suggestions for what to do better. However, they do need time, space, and a thought partner to reflect on their practice. Give them an opportunity to discuss strategies for continuing to grow in the profession. This may mean further refining their practice, stepping into leadership roles, or looking for ways to mentor others. Help them to self-identify areas they want to grow. We know a number of high-performing paraprofessionals who have gone on to become teachers. Each of them had supervisors who encouraged them. We all want to be on a continuous improvement journey, and for our superstar educators this is especially true.

Minor Tweaks Can Make a Major Difference

If you have a teacher who is effective and there is a small (or not so small) thing they could change, by all means–leverage the weight of the evaluation conference to help send that message. Tiffany was supporting a strong teacher who struggled with providing adequate wait time for her students. Tiffany shared this with the teacher after several observations, but it did not impact her practice. She decided to use this as the one area of improvement to raise during the end-of-year evaluation conference. By raising it in this high-stakes environment, it finally landed for the teacher. The next fall, the teacher got intentional with her wait time. Participation in discussions went up, more students had the opportunity to respond, and it significantly improved student outcomes.

Timing

Strategic scheduling of the final evaluation conferences is a must. It is very likely that staff will talk to one another about their conferences. This is not our favorite outcome, but it is to be expected, so we plan for it. If you know that a staff member is going to be upset about their conference and will share that information widely, plan to have other more positive conferences in the days prior or even that same day. When the staff member starts to vent about how critical you were in the conference, they won't find other staff members to commiserate with. When they see that they are the only ones who received negative feedback, it will only further highlight their need for improvement. You may also want to consider holding their conference at the end of the day or the week to minimize the people they will have access to. If you have a number of more negative conferences to hold, do your best to spread them out. This helps to avoid a situation where staff think that you are just an overly harsh evaluator, instead of thinking about how to improve their practice.

Connecting It

The evaluation process is one of the most high-leverage processes we have. Start with strong goals and support your staff in meeting them. Make sure you take the time to prepare for the final evaluation conference so it is impactful and effective. Choose the areas of focus and don't muddy the message by providing extraneous suggestions or information. Prepare the data and use it as a third point during the conference. Make sure you are crystal clear with your expectations and concerns. Carefully choose the timing of the conference based on the teacher's response to the feedback.

Connected Takeaways

- The evaluation process is one of the most high-leverage strategies for coaching up or coaching out.
- Suggestions during the evaluation conference are directives. Choose the area of focus carefully.
- What you share during the final evaluation conference has significant weight so leverage it.
- Don't forget your super star teachers.
- Choose the timing based on the teacher's response to feedback.

Conclusion

While writing this book, we had countless opportunities to reflect on some of the most challenging conversations we faced in school leadership. In doing so, we were struck by several things. One common thread was the significant emotional toll these conversations took on us. Another is that any regrets we have mostly stem from conversations that we waited too long to have or times that we shied away from a necessary conversation altogether. Although not every conversation went the way we wanted, we've learned that imperfect conversations are better than no conversations.

We've also realized that we are much stronger communicators because we've had one another. Throughout the years, and even still today, we call each other to talk through the trickiest conversations. We push each other to gain greater clarity of purpose, brainstorm key sentence frames, and at times we even practice the conversation. We are profoundly grateful to have one another as thought partners. We hope this book will provide that same support to you.

> Imperfect conversations are better than no conversations.

Being a strong communicator, especially when communicating the tough stuff, is a true skill. Just like any skill, it takes practice, dedication, and commitment to improve. As you embark on this journey, we encourage you to find a thought partner, or trusted coach. If you don't have that yet, reach out to us. No one should have to do this alone. As you continue to grow, give yourself grace. None of us will get it exactly right every time, but with reflection, every conversation will provide opportunity for growth.

This work is tough, but so are we. This doesn't mean that we are immune to escalated emotions when we do it. Do your best to take care of yourself by maintaining healthy practices and giving yourself space to recover. As you prepare to start the conversation, remember to drink water and remember to breathe. Not only will this keep you calm, but it will also sharpen your thinking. After the conversation, give yourself space to recover emotionally. Take a five-minute walk, close your eyes and breathe deeply, or take yourself to that space on campus that always lifts your spirits. Resist the urge to push through and dismiss your own emotions or needs. In order to engage in this work day after day, we must continue to refuel and be tender with ourselves.

Although difficult, the rewards of school leadership are also vast. There is something magical about seeing an educator blossom with the right coaching and direction. Recognizing the positive culture shift that emerges as negativity is confronted and extinguished is extraordinarily gratifying. And, of course, at the heart of it, is the joy of knowing our students are thriving under the care of exceptional educators.

With that, we thank you. We know you do not hear this nearly enough. Being a school leader is such hard and lonely work. Thank you for choosing it. Thank you for centering our students in all that you do, and for doing the right thing, even when it feels like the hardest thing. Thank you for engaging in tough conversations even when it's the last thing you

> At the very heart of education is connection.
>
> ———

want to do. Thank you for remembering that at the very heart of education is connection. Our children deserve leaders who bring out the best in all the educators who serve them, and you picked up this book to do just that.

We wrote this book to expand both your skill set and comfort with engaging in tough conversations so that you communicate with care, clarity, and confidence. If nothing else, we hope this book has helped you sleep a little better at night.

As you begin integrating this work into your tough conversations, let us know. We would love to welcome you to the Connected Communicator Movement. Join our community and explore the supportive tools, videos, free downloadable resources, and professional development offerings, on our website: www.ConnectingThroughConversation.com.

We are grateful to you. We are inspired by you. Thank you for doing your part to make our schools and the world a better place.

Appendices

Tough Conversation Planning Guide

Get Clear on the Goals: What do I want to get out of the conversation, and what do I want the other person to walk away with?

How, Where, When?

How will I communicate the message?	Where is the best location to have this conversation?	What time of day/day of the week will have the least impact on the other person's ability to work?

Email
   • Drop-by
   • Phone call
   • Scheduled
     meeting		

What needs to be communicated? List specific facts and details. Be as specific as possible. Include anything that must be said, even if it is difficult.

Consider any obstacles. What is your plan to overcome them?

Reminders & Tips

Ensure your motivation for the conversation stems from care. Stay focused on your goals for the conversation if things start to go off track. Watch for signs that you are trying to "win" or punish the other person out of anger. Be clear on action steps and summarize these at the end of the conversation and in writing. Above all, don't forget to breathe and stay calm.

~

Care Out Loud Routines

Build in regular routines to show how much you care about those you serve. These are a few that we have found to be effective in infusing care into your regular routine:

- **Making Rounds:** You may have heard the idea of managing by wandering around. A small twist on this idea is to intentionally schedule time into the beginning or end of the day to wander in and out of classrooms, the cafeteria, or joining recess for quick check-ins. Ask about their family, their hobbies, or if there is anything they need. The purpose is to build small talk into your day. When you come back at another time and check in about something you talked about, this shows that you see them, and you care about them personally. We recommend planning your route intentionally so that you are connecting with everyone over the course of a day or week, depending on the size of your campus.

As an added bonus, this will cut down significantly on your email, as a number of small things can be taken care of during these quick connections. Talk about a time saver!

- **Favorite Things:** Intentionally gathering the staff's favorite things is so useful! At the start of the year, find out everyone's favorite warm beverage, snack, hobbies, restaurants, books, and so on. Ask everyone to give you a work appropriate song they enjoy and use this to build a playlist for staff meetings. This is a fun way to make everyone feel a part of the group, and having folks guess who chose what song can be a great way to get to know each other better. When someone is having a rough day, showing up with their favorite coffee drink is a thoughtful way to demonstrate care. On their birthday, having a snack size bag of their favorite treats is personal and easy to do.

- **Celebrations and Shout-Outs:** Find ways to celebrate your staff, and help them celebrate each other. An easy way to do this is to start staff meetings with celebrations and shout-outs. A shout-out is someone calling out something they saw another educator do that is worth highlighting, and a celebration is something awesome that someone shares about themselves. We also love a shout-out board, where staff can write a shout-out to someone else and publicly display it. Whatever your system, just make sure there is a way to celebrate the great work being done.

- **Recognize Milestones:** Recognizing important events in people's lives shows you value them. Develop a system for celebrating everyone's birthday, no matter how old they are. After all, this is the only day every year that is all about them. Erika sets aside time on her calendar to write handwritten birthday cards for every staff member with a birthday that week. When someone has a major life event, such as a wedding, baby, graduation, etc., have a way to celebrate this. This doesn't have to fall only on you; we encourage you to establish a committee that is responsible for recognizing milestones. This can also be used when someone experiences a medical event or a loss. The committee ensures no one is forgotten and it becomes much more sustainable.

- **Strength Bombardment:** Have each staff member write their name on the top of a large piece of paper and place them around the room. Everyone goes to each paper and quietly writes something they appreciate about that person. The end result is a page of strengths and gratitudes that the person can take with them. This is such a meaningful exercise that makes the whole staff feel seen and connected. It is a wonderful way to end a school year. It's also an artifact that folks love to display in their offices or classrooms. Tiffany has led this exercise with students and staff alike. On more than one occasion, students have approached her years later and showed her their strength bombardment that they keep in their wallets as a constant reminder.

- **Intentional Greetings and Good-Byes:** As we know from working with students, the first and last part of any interaction is what is most likely to be remembered. The same is true for grown-ups. Take advantage of this to show care to each staff member as they enter a staff meeting by greeting them individually and by name. An easy way to do this is to meet them at the door and hand out the agenda so you can connect with everyone as they enter. This, combined with the staff playlist going in the background, starts every meeting with connection. When the meeting is over, try ending with a circle so each person can give a quick closing connection so everyone's voice is heard.

- **Play Together, Learn Together:** It is so important to laugh together as a staff. This lowers our affective filter, and makes us open to learning alongside each other. So, incorporate laughter. Put together quick Minute-to-Win-It games to get people laughing, ask "Would You Rather" questions, or use a silly activity (check out the appendix for easy no-prep icebreakers that will get people laughing). Share a meme or a funny thing a student said to start off a gathering. There are also times when you might organize a staff-wide scavenger hunt or group activity. This does not have to be expensive. A staff field day prior to school starting is so fun and it's free.

- **Celebrate the Good:** This may feel basic, but do not forget to say thank you. Find out how people like receiving praise. Then tailor how you show your thanks to match what is most meaningful to them. Some folks prefer private acknowledgements of gratitude. Others find a public thank you more meaningful. Everyone appreciates a handwritten note.

Framing It for Caregivers

Show Care: (Be genuine and specific about your care for their child)

What happened: (Share just the facts)

Why you think it happened: (Empathize or guess at motivation)

What happens next: (Share consequences or next steps)

Show care: (Remind them how much you care for their child)

Sentence Stems

We pulled sentence stems from throughout the book as a helpful go-to resource. To read more about applications, return to the chapter listed.

Solicit Feedback on Your Practice (Chapter 2)

- How can I better support you?
- Challenge my thinking on. . .
- I am struggling with x. Do you have any ideas how I could approach it more effectively?
- I would really appreciate your feedback on. . .
- I am feeling like I missed the mark in [that meeting, the presentation, a previous interaction]. Do you have feedback that could help me do better next time?

Responding to Requests for Confidential Information (Chapter 3)

- I wish I could share more information, but I can't for privacy reasons.

- I know you'd like me to tell you more about what's happening with that situation, but I really can't discuss that further, as it involves confidential staff information.
- I understand your curiosity, but that's not something I can share due to privacy laws and district policy.
- I have to protect confidentiality, so I can't go into details about that situation.
- I'm limited in what I can say about that because it concerns personnel matters.
- I can't comment on that specific situation, but I can share what our general process looks like.

Perspective Getting (Chapter 5)

- I'm curious how you feel about . . .
- What is running through your mind as I share this idea/issue/etc.?
- What has been your experience with . . .
- I would love your perspective on this.
- I could use a thought partner, what are you thinking about/feeling as we discuss this?

Getting to the Real Issue (Chapter 5)

- What would a resolution to this situation look like for you?
- How can I support you?
- What does support look like in this situation?
- What would be most helpful in order to move forward?

To Defuse (Chapter 8)

- This is super important.
- I am so glad you brought this concern to me.
- I am taking this very seriously.
- I am so sorry this happened.

Buying Time (Chapter 8)

- This conversation is really important. I want to make sure I can give it the time it deserves.
- I am committed to figuring out how we got here. I need some time to do some investigation so I have all the information we need to problem solve.
- This is too critical to be rushed. Let's schedule a time when we can problem-solve together.

Finding a Common Purpose (Chapter 8)

- How can I support you with this important issue?
- What does support look like in this situation?
- How can we move forward from here?
- We both want the same thing (the student's happiness/ safety/success, the class to be well managed, student behaviors to decrease, academic results to increase)
- Knowing we have the same goal, what can we do to get there in a way that will work for both of us?
- Thanks for partnering with me on this.

When Telling Your Story (Chapter 11)

- I am beginning to wonder . . .
- I'm starting to think . . .
- In my opinion . . .
- My perception is . . .
- Perhaps you were unaware of . . .

Wrapping Up a Meeting (Chapter 12)

- We need to be wrapping up now.
- At this point, we need to conclude.
- It is time to wrap this up.

Supporting Goal Setting

- If the goal is too vague
  - How will you know if you've met this goal by the end of the year?
  - What specific student outcomes will show progress?
  - Can we make this measurable so we can track growth?
- If the goal lacks rigor
  - Does this target push student learning far enough?
  - What would this goal look like if we raised expectations to match grade-level standards?
  - If all students met this goal, would it significantly move our SIP targets?
- If the goal doesn't align to schoolwide priorities
  - How does this goal connect to our PLC or SIP priorities?

- What adjustments could we make so your goal reinforces the team's focus?
  - How might aligning this goal with our schoolwide fluency focus give your students extra support?
- If the teacher needs support in instruction, management, or culture
  - What strategies would help bring more clarity to your instruction?
  - How can your goal support consistent classroom management routines?
  - What steps could you take to strengthen classroom positivity and relationships?

Probing Questions for Coaching Out (Chapter 15)

- How are you going to make significant improvements?
- How do you feel about your performance?
- Are you happy in this position?
- Do you feel effective?
- Are you feeling like this job is a good match for your skill set?
- What do you see as a path forward?

References

Bare, E., & Burns, T. (2023). *Connecting through conversation: A playbook for talking with students.* ConnectEDD Publishing.

Brown, B. (2018). *Dare to lead.* Vermilion.

Bryk, A., & Schneider, B. (2002). Trust in schools: A core resource for improvement. New York: Russell Sage Foundation.

Collins, J. (2005). *Built to last - successful habits of visionary companies.* Arrow Books Ltd.

Covey, S. M. R. (2008). *The Speed of trust: The one thing that changes everything.* Simon & Schuster.

Duhigg, C. (2024). *Supercommunicators.* Random House.

Gruenert, S., & Whitaker, T. (2015). *School culture rewired: How to define, assess, and transform it.* ASCD.

Hammond, Z. (2015). *Culturally responsive teaching and the brain: Promoting authentic engagement and rigor among culturally and linguistically diverse students.* Corwin Press.

Jackson, L. (2002). *Freaks, geeks & asperger syndrome: A user guide to Adolescence.* Jessica Kingsley Publishers.

Lipton, L., & Wellman, B. (2018). *Learning-focused supervision.* Corwin.

Maxwell, J. C. (2014). *Good leaders ask great questions: Your foundation for successful leadership.* Center Street.

Mehrabian, A. (1971). *Silent messages.* Wadsworth.

Paterson, K., Grenny, J., McMillan, R., & Switzler, A. (2012). *Crucial conversations: Tools for talking when Stakes are high* (2nd ed.). McGraw-Hill.

Pilcher, J. (2023). *Hardwiring excellence in education: The nine principles® framework.* Studer Education.

Scott, K. (2017). *Radical candor: Be a kick-ass boss without losing your humanity.* St. Martin's Press.

Stone, D., Patton, B., & Heen, S. (1999). *Difficult conversations: How to discuss what matters most.* Penguin Books.

Winerman, L. (2005, October). The mind's mirror: A new type of neuron—called a mirror neuron—could help explain how we learn through mimicry and why we empathize with others. *Monitor on Psychology, 36*(9), 48.

Acknowledgements

The creation of this book would not have been possible without the countless mentors, teachers, and guides we have been so fortunate to have along the way. There is a fear in listing them, as we are sure to leave someone out. Instead, we would like to thank every colleague who ever acted as a thought partner or helped us through a problem of practice. You made us better. Every supervisor we have worked with has provided so many lessons, and to you we are grateful. For those of you who have mentored us, coached us, taught us, and guided us, your impact on us is profound. Thank you all.

To those of you who read early versions of our manuscript and provided meaningful feedback and extraordinary tremendous insight, our book is stronger because of you. Thank you.

This work would not have been possible without the tremendous support of our families. Their endless encouragement and love kept us going, especially when we were not sure we wanted to. Thank you.

Finally, thank you to the team at ConnectEDD for elevating our work and helping us to make it great.

About the Authors

Erika Bare has been an educator for over twenty years, currently serving as a superintendent in Oregon. She began her career as a special educator teaching students pre-k through 21 before becoming a building administrator serving at both the high school and elementary level. She then expanded her impact as the director of special education & assistant superintendent before moving into her current position as superintendent. She is passionate about supporting all students through individual supports to reach their unlimited potential. Erika's greatest joy comes in spending time with her extremely supportive husband and two remarkable children. Their time together is made sweeter by an energetic dog, and three very mischievous cats.

Tiffany **Burns** loves working with kids and their grownups. With over two decades in education, she has taught elementary, middle, and high school students in public, private, bilingual, and homeschool settings across Oregon, Alaska, and Mexico. She has served as a school administrator since 2012–including nine years as an elementary school principal. After years leading schools, Tiffany is thrilled to be back in the classroom, teaching in the School of Education at Southern Oregon University and providing leadership coaching to school and district leaders. Tiffany is passionate about improving instruction, strengthening behavior systems, and building sustainable structures that support strong teaching, cultures of connection, and high expectations that honor children's potential and their humanity. Tiffany lives in the Siskiyou Mountains with her college sweetheart husband, their two fabulous children, and a huge and fairly ridiculous dog.

Erika and Tiffany connected in 2011 in their administrative licensure program. They bonded over a shared passion for students and the educators who serve them. They enjoy collaborating and writing as a way to share their expertise with other educators. Most recently, they published *Connecting Through Conversation: A Playbook for Talking with Students*. You can find it, along with many free resources, on their website www.connectingthroughconversation.com. Erika and Tiffany love supporting educators through professional development, consultation, and facilitation of book studies with educators across the country. At the heart of their work—and the mission of Connecting Through Conversation—is a deep commitment to ensuring that all students feel loved, understood, and experience a deep sense of belonging so they learn and grow at the highest levels.

More from ConnectEDD Publishing

Since 2015, ConnectEDD has worked to transform education by empowering educators to become better-equipped to teach, learn, and lead. What started as a small company designed to provide professional learning events for educators has grown to include a variety of services to help educators and administrators address essential challenges. ConnectEDD offers instructional and leadership coaching, professional development workshops focusing on a variety of educational topics, a roster of nationally recognized educator associates who possess hands-on knowledge and experience, educational conferences custom-designed to meet the specific needs of schools, districts, and state/national organizations, and ongoing, personalized support, both virtually and onsite. In 2020, ConnectEDD expanded to include publishing services designed to provide busy educators with books and resources consisting of practical information on a wide variety of teaching, learning, and leadership topics. Please visit us online at connecteddpublishing.com or contact us at: info@connecteddpublishing.com

Recent Publications:

Live Your Excellence: Action Guide by Jimmy Casas

Culturize: Action Guide by Jimmy Casas

Daily Inspiration for Educators: Positive Thoughts for Every Day of the Year by Jimmy Casas

Eyes on Culture: Multiply Excellence in Your School by Emily Paschall

Pause. Breathe. Flourish. Living Your Best Life as an Educator by William D. Parker

L.E.A.R.N.E.R. Finding the True, Good, and Beautiful in Education by Marita Diffenbaugh

Educator Reflection Tips Volume II: Refining Our Practice by Jami Fowler-White

Handle With Care: Managing Difficult Situations in Schools with Dignity and Respect by Jimmy Casas and Joy Kelly

Disruptive Thinking: Preparing Learners for Their Future by Eric Sheninger

Permission to be Great: Increasing Engagement in Your School by Dan Butler

Daily Inspiration for Educators: Positive Thoughts for Every Day of the Year, Volume II by Jimmy Casas

The 6 Literacy Levers: Creating a Community of Readers by Brad Gustafson

The Educator's ATLAS: Your Roadmap to Engagement by Weston Kieschnick

In This Season: Words for the Heart by Todd Nesloney, LaNesha Tabb, Tanner Olson, and Alice Lee

Leading with a Humble Heart: A 40-Day Devotional for Leaders by Zac Bauermaster

Recalibrate the Culture: Our Why…Our Work…Our Values by Jimmy Casas

Creating Curious Classrooms: The Beauty of Questions by Emma Chiappetta

Crafting the Culture: 45 Reflections on What Matters Most by Joe Sanfelippo and Jeffrey Zoul

Improving School Mental Health: The Thriving School Community Solution by Charle Peck and Dr. Cameron Caswell

Building Authenticity: A Blueprint for the Leader Inside You by Todd Nesloney and Tyler Cook

Connecting Through Conversation: A Playbook for Talking with Students by Erika Bare and Tiffany Burns

The Dream Factory: Designing a Purposeful Life by Mark Trumbo

Stories Behind Stances: Creating Empathy Through Hearing "The Other Side" by Chris Singleton

Happy Eyes: Becoming All Things to All People by Ryan Tillman

The Generative Age: Artificial Intelligence and the Future of Education by Alana Winnick

Recalibrate the Culture: Action Guide by Jimmy Casas

Leading with PEOPLE: A Six Pillar Framework for Fruitful Leadership by Zac Bauermaster

A School Leader's Guide to Reclaiming Purpose by Frederick C. Buskey

Foundations of an Elite Culture: Building Success with High Standards and a Positive Environment by David Arencibia

Personalize: Meeting the Needs of All Learners by Eric Sheninger and Nicki Slaugh

The Five Principles of Educator Professionalism: Rebuilding Trust in Schools by Nason Lollar

Words on the Wall: Culturizing Your Classroom For Observable Impact by Jimmy Casas and Cale Birk

School of Engagement: 45 Activities to Ignite Student Learning by Jonathan Alsheimer

Intentional Instructional Moves: Strategic Steps to Accelerate Student Learning by Sherry St. Clair

Overcoming Education: Complex Challenges, Difficult People, and the Art of Making a Difference by Brad R. Gustafson

The Language of Behavior: A Framework to Elevate Student Success by Charle Peck and Joshua Stamper

Whose Permission Are You Waiting For? An Educator's Guide to Doing What You Love by William D. Parker

The Leader You're Not…And Why It's Just As Important As the Leader You Are by Scott Borba

The Growth-Minded Leader by Tyler Cook

Day by Day: 180 Days of Hope and Encouragement by Zac Bauermaster

Make Your Move: For Ambitious People Ready to Live Their Aspirations by Marlon Styles, Jr.

The Hidden Work: What Separates Top Performers From Underachievers by Weston Kieschnick

Lifted to Lead: How a Paraplegic Orphan Rose from the Streets of Saigon to Become an American Leader by Stefan Bean and Kathy Nash

Lead From Who You Are: The Personal, People, and Process Rhythms of Meaningful Leadership by Joe Sanfelippo

Ready to Lead with AI: A Practical Guide for School Leaders by Kip Glazer

When All Means All: The Constellation of Learning Approach to Student-Centered Schools by Adam D. Drummond-Konopasek and Danny Drummond-Konopasek